90-222383
B
Graham
7
45
Graham, Maury
Iron r
s kin
1995
W9-CFY-226
ORANGE COUNTY LIBRARY SYSTEM
27

TALES OF THE IRON ROAD

TALES OF THE IRON ROAD

My Life as King of the Hobos

"Steam Train" MAURY GRAHAM
and ROBERT J. HEMMING

PARAGON HOUSE
NEW YORK

First edition, 1990
Published in the United States by
Paragon House
90 Fifth Avenue
New York, NY 10011

Copyright © 1990 by Robert J. Hemming

All rights reserved. No part of this book may be reproduced, in any form, without written permission from the publishers, unless by a reviewer who wishes to quote brief passages.

90-222883

Designed by Deirdre C. Amthor
Manufactured in the United States of America

Library of Congress Cataloging-in-Publication Data

Graham, Maury
Tales of the iron road: my life as king of the hobos/"Steam Train" by Maury Graham and Robert J. Hemming.—1st ed.
p. cm.
Includes index.
ISBN 1-55778-129-X: $19.95
1. Graham, Maury. 2. Tramps—United States—Biography.
I. Hemming, Robert J. II. Title.
HV4505.G83 1990
305.5'68—dc20
[B] 89-8682
CIP

The paper used in this publication meets the minimum requirements of American National Standard for Information Sciences—Permanence of Paper for Printed Library Materials, ANSIZ39.48-1984.

Second printing

In loving memory
of Janet Rose Hemming
who was never to know
what she had started.

TABLE OF CONTENTS

Contents

ACKNOWLEDGMENTS

An established custom in the literary world dictates that at some point in a book such as this, credit should be extended to those who have contributed to the research, writing, editing and publishing of the work.

I would like to modify that custom to a slight degree or, perhaps, to a major degree. Rather than expressing my gratitude to the individuals who assisted me in writing this book, I would like to publicly thank some of the people who helped me live it.

There are many individuals without whose kind and generous assistance I could not possibly have survived as a hobo, could not have lived long enough to have a story to tell or the ability to tell it. There almost certainly will be those who deserve mention here but who, because of editing considerations or a lack of space or, more likely, my careless memory, will have been overlooked. I pray they will forgive the oversight and understand my human failing.

The one who most deserves to be mentioned first is my brother, James Graham, who took me on my first road trip. Hoboing was in my blood from that time; it is doubtful that I would have had the life I did without Jim's introduction to traveling and living out in the open.

Father John Brickley, of Britt, Iowa, our National Hobo Chaplain, has a special fondness for the men and women of the road. Father John has done much for hobos, myself included. He prays for all vagabonds, regardless of their religious denomination. He has certainly earned a place on the tail of Halley's comet for a ride through the solar system before he enters the pearly gates.

Many fine people over the years have helped me along the road, giving me rides when walking was becoming an impossible chore, taking me into their homes for warmth and comfort and feeding me when I was hungry. It isn't possible to list—or even to recall—all of them. The following are but a few of those I most remember.

Cliff and Shirlee Peterson of Mt. Vernon, Iowa, took me into their home one terrible freezing night and possibly saved my life. They have been dear friends since, as have David Schisiler and his parents, Short and Betty Schisiler; Maurice Steidinger; Dave and Marge Miller of Logansport, Indiana; Ed and Sharon Schrof of Forest, Illinois, and George Wireman of Thurmont, Maryland. Jim Burns, who owns a restaurant in West Chicago, Illinois, was always good to me and other hobos. He is a great barbecue man. Robert McCain of Monticello, Indiana, Russ Garms of Cedar Rapids, Iowa, and Harold and Ethel Hoppe of Walcott, Indiana, have also demonstrated a great charity and compassion and made me feel welcome in their homes on many occasions.

Some of the many others who have treated me kindly and inspired me during my travels include: Cadet Thorpe, chief of police in Sterling, Illinois, who always

took very good care of me whenever I passed through; Tom Hill of Ottawa, Illinois, whose love for steam engines developed into a collector's hobby (he bought an old brickyard where he could store the engines he found and purchased, and welcomed me whenever I was in town); former Norfolk and Western fireman Joe Ciesielski of McDonald, Pennsylvania; L. K. Penninggroth of New Athens, Illinois, who saved a beautiful railroad depot from destruction, then had it dismantled and moved to his property where it was fully restored; and Dennis O'Conner of Grand Junction, Colorado, who was one of the kindest railroad men I ever met. The wonderful people who run the Hobo Committee at South Dakota State University in Brookings, South Dakota, deserve great credit. They've held Hobo Day ever since 1911; it's always held on Homecoming Weekend and draws probably the largest crowd of *any* state function held on an annual basis. These people are dedicated to making the weekend a total success and have never failed. I would also like to thank H. B. Chambers and Fred Graham of the Kennedy Space Center who listened so patiently to my fears of a rocket flying through Halley's comet.

Bruce Watrol of Maumee, Ohio, deserves special mention. He is a gifted artist who has portrayed the hobo in drawings and paintings and has used his talent to make society more aware of the hobo. Boxcar Willie, a well-known country and western singer, has also done a lot to elevate the hobo in the public's esteem. It was his dedication to the hobo's cause that earned him the title Hobo Ambassador. December Lee of Tonapah, Nevada, has also contributed much through her many fine poems about hobos and vagabonds. Benita Stankey—also known as Slow-Motion Ben—has earned the gratitude of all hobos tenderly caring for the unknown hobo's grave in Lamont, Iowa, for almost 70 years.

I have objected on the rare occasion when a news reporter or editor would sarcastically refer to me as the "self-styled king of the hobos," the "self-appointed king of the hobos" or the individual "claiming to be king of the hobos." I always felt that if they held me in such low repute they should not have referred to me at all. But they always printed the story about me and were interested enough in what I had to say to want to quote me. It seemed to me that this was unprofessional and hypocritical. Fortunately, these instances have been few. The vast majority of the press have been very interested, kind, considerate and helpful in my attempts to get word about the hobo out to the public. Among these members of the press have been: Ann Orth, a wonderful reporter formerly with the *Corn Belt Press;* Barbara Chapman who wrote for a number of papers in Illinois and who always treated me with respect and kindness; Hank Harvey of the Toledo *Blade,* who is responsible for my road name; Sally Vallongo, also of the *Blade,* who wrote a very sensitive story about my wife, Wanda; Willard Scott of NBC's *Today* show; Don Lazadder of the Indianapolis *Star;* Dan Carlinsky of the *New York Times,* Tim Elledge of the *Fort Worth Press;* Charles Kuralt of CBS; and the staffs of hundreds of newspapers around the country who continue to write about the hobo and his life but who aren't given bylines to their stories.

I owe a special thanks to the staffs of the television news departments at Channels 11, 13 and 24 in Toledo for the many kind stories they've broadcast about me over the years; and a special thanks to John Kelly and Marilyn Turner, hosts of *Kelly and Company* on Detroit's WXYZ-TV. Paul W. Smith of radio station WMCA in New York also has my appreciation for his efforts to educate the public about the hobo.

There are whole communities in this great country who have labored to keep the spirit of the hobo alive and who have inspired and encouraged me over the years. The people of Amory, Mississippi, Logansport, Indiana, Durand, Michigan, Dows, Iowa, Thurmont, Maryland, Brookings, South Dakota and Toledo, Ohio, are just a

few. And of course I could not overlook the people of Britt, Iowa, who have made the hobo feel welcome and special for nearly a century.

With all the assistance I've received from so many fine people around the country, it may seem strange that I worry that the memory of the hobo might fade. However, there are so many who have not yet heard the story of the "gentleman of the road" that I feel I must continue spreading the word.

I would not have survived my first trip on the freights had it not been for a number of old 'bos I met in Toledo and got to know well. They taught me the history of the hobos and taught me how to stay alive on the road. I can't remember all of their names, but a few were: Maumee Kid, Maumee Boy, River Bank, Crick Bank, Tin Can, Stones (he always carried stones to put in his hobo stew), Fossil Head, and Catfish Eddy. They were my sponsors, my teachers and my dear friends.

In 1981 I wandered into a summer camp for kids just west of Toledo. They were sitting around a camp fire and I thought that I might make their evening a bit more enjoyable by telling them something about hobos and nature and the joy of the great outdoors. One of the kids was a dear little girl who was impressed enough by my talk to ask her daddy if he thought I would be willing to come to her school and talk to her classmates about hoboing. He said that it was worth asking her teacher about. She did, the teacher thought it was a grand idea and contacted me to extend an invitation. I love my appearances before schoolchildren and my visit to Toledo's St. Ann's school was especially pleasant. I made the little girl who had been responsible for the invitation a Princess of the Hobos for her services in spreading the hobo word to other children. Her daddy called her princess from that day on.

The little girl's name was Janet Rose Hemming and her daddy was an author of nonfiction books. After several years of talking with Bob Hemming about collaborating on a book about my experiences on the "iron road," I finally agreed.

Sadly though, Janet Rose wasn't able to share in the pleasure we experienced working on this project. On March 27, 1985—almost two years before we began work on this book—Janet died of the effects of cystic fibrosis. She was sixteen. But I'm sure she knows about it and I hope she's looking down with satisfaction and pride. It was through her interest and effort that many more people will come to know about hobos and what made them such a national historical treasure, and it is for that reason this book is dedicated to Janet's memory.

Acknowledging the help and support I've received during my hobo years would not be complete without mentioning my dear daughters, Alice and Karen. I've always been intensely proud of my girls, both of whom became registered nurses, wives and mothers. I've always been aware that, while they loved me dearly, they weren't always proud of my behavior. Nor, I suppose have their husbands, Marvin Spangler and Terry Carson. Still, I believe I'm an extremely lucky man to have two wonderful daughters and two fine sons. They have helped me greatly and I am forever grateful for their love and support. I'm very proud of them.

Finally, I wish to thank the one person who is most responsible for everything worthwhile I may have accomplished in my life on the road, the person who sacrificed the most on my behalf, the one who always held out a belief that perhaps I really could amount to something someday. If I have, it's because of her efforts, her prayers and her love. I owe it all to my beloved wife, Wanda. I hope she will always believe it's been worth it.

INTRODUCTION

Lying tight against the old Chicago Northwestern railroad line, running west from Chicago across the flat, verdant heartland of America, is Lamont, Iowa, a farming community of about 2,100. A hobo got killed in a train wreck there in the early 1920s. He had no identification on him and no one knew his name. As an act of gentle charity by the quiet, compassionate people of Lamont, the unknown hobo was buried in one corner of the small, tree-shaded cemetery located near the rail line on the outskirts of town.

But the grave was unmarked and several young girls from nearby farms were particularly touched by the sad vision of the nameless, unmourned man, placed beneath the sod for all eternity without so much as a stone to mark where he slept. Searching the area for an appropriate grave marker, they found a neatly cut piece of bridge stone, flat and of a proper size. It had a hole drilled through the side—probably for some kind of pin or fastener. The girls felt the hole offered an ideal place in which to put freshly cut wild flowers that grew in abundance in nearby fields.

Benita Stankey was one of those girls. She remembers that they installed the stone at the head of the man's grave with the drilled side facing skyward and placed buttercups and daisies and black-eyed Susans in the hole. It looked so nice, she recalls, that they vowed to continue placing flowers there as long as they could. That was sixty-seven years ago and the flowers continue appearing at the old hobo's grave to this day; the tradition has been carried on by the girls' daughters and granddaughters.

Yet, in spite of the loving care that has been shown his grave over the years, it is not unlikely that, had he known of his imminent demise, the unknown hobo would have asked to be buried 119 miles northwest of Lamont, in Britt, Iowa.

Britt, about the same size as Lamont, is located in the north-central part of the state, twenty miles or so below the Minnesota line, and has for nearly a century been a favorite stopping-off point for those who traveled the "iron road."

The town has always been a friendly, warm place for hobos who found they were able to share with these genial people a mutual respect and an honest regard for each other that vagabonds found hard to match anywhere else. Because of this kinship, the hobos made Britt, Iowa, their official capital.

Today, Britt is the scene of an annual gathering—the National Hobo Convention—held the first week of August each year. One of the ceremonies conducted during the seven-day event is a memorial service at the town cemetery. There, in "Hobos' Row," are buried the remains of hobos who have chosen endless slumber in that cemetery, near the kindly people of Britt who had always made them welcome.

In life, they had come to this hamlet, as most hobos did, uninvited and unexpected, and like the unknown hobo, they had taken from the good people of this area only a few wild flowers and some tender affection, asking of them just a small, quiet place in which to lay their heads and rest for a short while.

Now, in death, those on Hobo's Row will rest in their small, quiet place for all time.

I understand the hobos' deep feeling for Britt and its citizens; I spent close to twenty years riding freight trains, hoboing in almost every part of the country. I was five times elected King of the Hobos in ceremonies conducted in Britt during the annual Hobo Convention and have been awarded the permanent title, Hobo King of the East. As one of them, I'm aware that the hobo is a doomed species that will soon vanish forever.

In my years of travel as the hobos' king, I've made it my special mission to proselytize the hobo philosophy of kindness and compassion, of courtesy, trust and concern for man and nature.

What follows is the chronicle of my life and my travels. It is also the story of hoboing as I knew it, and of the hobos I've known.

It is all true.

I want now to tell my story in the hope that through these "tales of the iron road" the reader will come to know the hobo as the residents of Britt have known him; that society might gain an understanding of the hobo and what he contributed to mankind; that from my experiences, and those of other hobos I've known, there will develop an appreciation of the marvelous historical treasure the American hobo has become; that this awareness will insure that the spirit of the unknown hobo will forever be at peace; and that the legacy of every hobo who ever took to the iron road will be preserved.

"Steam Train" Maury Graham

TALES OF THE IRON ROAD

CHAPTER 1

A LONESOME TIME

In June of 1931—as Maurice W. Graham—I climbed aboard my first boxcar and headed west. I was fourteen years old and, without realizing it, had just taken the first step to becoming an authentic hobo.

Forty-nine years and uncounted miles later—now known as "Steam Train" Maury—I was, for the final time, huddled in a boxcar again heading west . . . and hoboing was over for me.

A chronic love of the outdoors and a restless inner prodding had sent me on the road at a tender age, and after nearly a half century my deteriorating physical condition was doing what neither the brutal elements nor the constant dangers nor the unfriendly railroad police could do. I was being forced out of a way of life I had loved with an indescribable passion.

During the last years on the road I suffered severe, almost constant pain caused by a degenerating bone problem in my hip that produced an incipient limp and made walking long distances all but unbearable.

The cold, damp days and nights outdoors, which in my younger years had never bothered me, were now terribly uncomfortable. Sleeping on the ground had become an agony I could hardly endure.

And the relentless passage of time had robbed me of speed; I was no longer as fast nor as surefooted as I once had been. In the past few years I'd found it increasingly difficult to climb aboard the moving cars of the freight trains I rode around the country.

It was undeniable; the seductive "iron road" on which I'd ridden so many miles couldn't go on forever for me. The end of the line was in sight.

But, while my long career as a hobo was ending, the loss of this way of life probably shouldn't have saddened me all that much; there was so little left of the old days, the "hobo jungles" that had dotted the river banks along trackside had vanished, and there were few hobos left to use them.

First to go had been the steam locomotive, the formidable steel monster that had chugged and moaned and groaned and belched ugly, sooty smoke, the black beast that was always called "she" or "lady" and was loved passionately by everyone connected in any way with railroading.

Then the railroads themselves began disappearing, their strength sapped, their purpose plundered by the automobile and the truck and the jet plane.

Now it was the turn of the hobos, relics of a bygone era, for whom there was no place in the modern world. We have pretty much all gone from the freight yards and riverbanks of America. Our numbers are being rapidly depleted; soon there will be none of us left and we will have taken with us a special part of this country's past.

Embarking on what I knew would be my last ride on

the freights filled me with a profound sadness. Giving up the free life didn't come easy. Memories of the adventures I'd experienced through years of traveling the "high iron" washed over me, memories of the hobos I'd met and come to know, men with colorful names, names like Fry-Pan Jack, Slow-Motion Shorty, Hood River Blackie, The Hard Rock Kid and Galway Slim. And the women, like Boxcar Bertha and Liz Lump (the first black hobo queen) and Hobo Josie, who rode freight trains with her husband.

There were warm, happy memories of quiet afternoons by pleasant streams and of nights in hobo camps, seated around a bright fire, exchanging stories and songs and adventures with other hobos. To be sure, there were unpleasant memories, too, memories of bitterly cold weather, of snow and sleet, of trying to sleep on the frigid ground in a bedroll soaked in slush or drenched in driving rains. There were memories of stifling days in overheated boxcars, of hunger and pain. And there were frightening memories of the "bulls," the brutal, sadistic railroad police who patrolled the freight yards, preying on hapless wanderers; and grim memories of being imprisoned in dirty city and county jails and pressed into work gangs to be sold like a slave to farmers to harvest their crops.

It was a life that hobos had led throughout their history. Yet, in spite of the dangers, the degradation and deprivation, they had flourished. From the end of the Civil War through the Great Depression of the 1930s and afterward, thousands of hobos had roamed the corridors created by the railroads that crisscrossed the nation.

They had lived their carefree lives, traveling the country on "zero dollars a day," occasionally touching those they met with quiet, unassuming gentleness, passing the days, waiting for that time when they would hear the call of the "Westbound," the hobo's lingo for death. Now, most were gone; they'd caught the Westbound.

While, for more than a century, there were countless numbers of men and women wandering throughout the

United States and Canada, riding freight trains wherever they could climb aboard them, the hobos of North America were a particularly unique institution. They were a strict society that lived by a narrow code of conduct and accepted applications for membership cautiously. Not everyone who decided to forsake the traditional American work ethic of the "home guard" was or could be a hobo.

The reasons people became hobos were as varied as the reasons people became doctors or lawyers or ministers . . . or nothing at all. My reasons had a great deal to do with a lonely, often unhappy, childhood.

• • •

I was born in Atchison, Kansas, on June 3, 1917, almost as a parental afterthought—I was fourteen years younger than my sister Alice—the fourth and last child of Andy and Carrie Craft Graham.

My grandparents had come from Scotland in the 1800s to settle around Atchison, Kansas. After a few years there, my grandfather, John Graham, had followed the forty-niners to California during the great gold rush of the mid-nineteenth century. He didn't strike it rich, but returned with a pair of magnificent six-shooters, complete with finely hand-tooled leather belt and holsters. He was able to trade this prize for a small farm about eight miles outside of town.

Times were extremely hard back then; gravestones found at the farm indicated that about six of my distant relatives died in their teens and early twenties, probably from influenza. Eventually, most of the Graham and Craft clans migrated west, settling in Idaho and Washington.

My father was a carpenter/home builder; my mother was a nurse. In 1924, mother contracted a debilitating form of encephalitis which ultimately turned her into a hopeless invalid, trapped in a failing body, prevented from giving me the sensitive, loving attention her motherly instincts cried out to provide. When I was eight years old, my dad, prodded by a sense of desperation—watching mother's worsening condition and realizing that it would soon be impossible for her to fulfill the simplest obligations to my care decided to send me away to live with relatives.

Over the next five years I was shuttled from family to family, first to the farm of Ernest and Goldie Maxted, an aunt and uncle. From my first day with them it was clear that I was there as a farmhand and little else. Life on the farm was exhausting and demanding for a little boy. The Maxteds, like most farmers in the area, raised a variety of crops on their small place: wheat, corn, hay and alfalfa. They grew vegetables for family use and for the produce markets in Atchison. Every minute of daylight was a precious resource to be used productively; everyone worked and I was expected to earn my keep, to give a full day's labor in the fields shocking wheat, hay and corn. There were fruit trees to be tended and harvested, firewood and corncobs to be carried to the woodbox each day; the stock had to be fed and watered, chickens fed and eggs gathered; the chicken coop and stables had to be cleaned regularly, and, in winter, I had to attend school, walking in rain and snow and ice and mud to the one-room schoolhouse three miles away.

There was little time for an eight-year-old boy to enjoy boyhood pursuits. But at every opportunity I would sneak off to nearby Walnut Creek, a shallow stream running through the farm that had a number of deep holes where I found I could catch the nicest bluegills and sunfish I'd ever seen. Whenever Aunt Goldie or Uncle Ernest caught me going to the creek they'd beat me proper. But it never stopped me from going.

Fishing in Walnut Creek was one of the few happy experiences I enjoyed during my stay on the farm. Another was the weekly trip to town.

Traditionally, Saturday nights were the "big night" for farmers, the time when the week's work was done and everyone could relax and cut loose a bit, the night when the family would go into town to buy the next week's supplies and stand on street corners or in the brightly lighted shops to gossip with friends.

We'd hitch the team to the wagon and all go into Atchison. It was a very pleasant thing for me because I would get to see my mom and dad and some of my other relatives. The other nights of the week, particularly in the winter, were dull and tedious. Everyone would go to bed very early so that they could get up very early the next morning. There wasn't much else to do. On the rare occasions when people came to visit, we'd gather in the parlor where Aunt Goldie would play the piano and we would sing spirituals and gospel songs.

I shared a bedroom with my younger cousin Edward, a depraved little tyrant whose worldly purpose seemed to be making my life unbearable. I sometimes think that everyone has a cousin Edward. Mine grew up to be a fine man. But when he was a kid he was the meanest stinker that ever was.

When his ma and pa weren't looking, he would bite and pinch and otherwise assault me, and if I tried to defend myself, he would run and tell Aunt Goldie that I'd slapped him. I didn't dare lay a hand on him. If I did, I got a whipping, and I mean they'd *whip* me. They thought their little darling was incapable of doing wrong.

Eventually, the chance for sweet revenge came along.

We had a big old billy goat on the farm and I found out how to make that goat madder than hell; I'd get him by the horns and shake him and kick him on the nose, and he'd get so mad he could butt down a tree. When I got him real stirred up, I'd point him at Edward and turn him loose. He'd butt that kid end over apple cart, and stomp him with his front feet to boot; he'd skin that kid up something awful. Then, after he'd given him a good going over, I'd rush in and "rescue" him and take him in the house. I was a hero, I'd "done rescued the kid." With a perfectly straight face I'd tell them, "That goat's gonna kill him one of these days."

If I felt miserable living with these relatives, *they* weren't all that pleased with having me there. Assuming the responsibility for someone else's child, even a close relative's, became a burdensome obligation they eventually felt unwilling to continue. At age nine, after a year on the farm, I was shuttled back to my parents.

Leaving the farm meant giving up my beloved woods and the quiet moments along Walnut Creek. But life back in Atchison was not without its pleasures; I enjoyed cat fishing along the wooded banks and back waters of the Missouri River, and shooting marbles with a rich kid who had buckets of them in his garage. I lived a kind of Huck Finn life there. But the family environment was not destined to be a secure and happy one for me. Nor was it to be long-lived.

Dad attempted to carry on as father and husband, but work for him was scarce in Atchison and he began traveling in search of building projects. His long absences placed a strain on family life and the marriage began to crumble. He found work in Toledo, Ohio, helping to build the Commodore Perry Hotel, a plush downtown landmark that continued into the 1970s as one of the city's finest inns. In 1929, he decided to stay in Toledo . . . permanently. He also decided to take unto himself another wife and family. Mother and Dad were divorced.

I didn't know, at the time, that my parents were divorcing; in my confused state of mind, I thought the family was breaking up because of mother's illness, that Dad had to be able to move around easily to find work and mother simply was not well enough to keep up. To an eleven-year-old, it made sense that she should be with her kin where she could be properly cared for.

My sister Lulu, who was six years older than I, eventually went to Toledo to live with Dad and his new family. Mother, my sister Alice and I moved to Emmet, Idaho, to live with her mother and the other relatives who had settled here.

The move west meant living with yet another aunt and

uncle and being separated from mother again. But this time there were some really pleasant aspects that helped ease the hurt and loneliness: the Idaho high country and the close companionship with a trio of friendly cousins, Ralph, Alton and Max Heath. They taught me to ride horses and shared with me the wild, unspoiled outdoors that was the western United States in the 1920s, making life seem brighter and filled with new adventures.

The cousins were the product of Uncle John Heath's first marriage to an American Indian of the Nez Percé tribe. They taught me about some of the Indian culture and tradition and about the glories of living off the land.

There was time for fun, but I was also required to earn my keep and had to work as hard as I played. In addition to the usual farm chores I was pressed into service helping with the various harvests in the fertile Idaho farm and ranch country. I labored in the hay fields, picked cherries, apricots, peaches, pears and apples as well as the famous Idaho potatoes.

But, as it had been with the other places I'd lived, it didn't last long. When the harvests were over there was no great need for an eleven-year-old boy. I was sent away again, this time to Seattle, Washington, to live with my brother Jim and his wife and small child. From the beginning, I didn't like living there; it was city living and I was, by this time, hopelessly addicted to the great outdoors.

The adjustment to another home and family was never fully made and most of the memories of that time have mercifully been erased. What I can recall is that within a year it became apparent that the situation in Seattle would not be any more permanent than it had been in Atchison or Emmet. Times were bad, Jim was a house builder like my dad, and business wasn't good. He was also having marital problems.

As soon as school recessed for the summer Jim told me I'd have to go back to Idaho. He couldn't afford to send me by bus so he decided he'd take me back by hitchhiking. It was a wonderful trip for me. We slept in straw stacks and barns, living a free kind of life. We worked small jobs along the way, picking fruit and helping to harvest other crops to make some money along the way. Jim shingled a couple of barn roofs and I helped as best I could carrying the cedar shingles up to him. We met many interesting people on that trip and the excitement of this new and wonderful adventure had a profound effect on my future life.

It took between ten days and two weeks to make the trip, and I enjoyed every minute of it. I realize now that it posed a great hardship for Jim; he had to get back and make a living, and he had his marital troubles to worry about. But he accepted a sense of responsibility toward me and never complained.

When we finally arrived in Emmet, he said his good-byes and left quickly for the long trip back, having done as much as he could for me. I hated to see him go, and I wasn't sure when I'd ever see him again. But I was back in the only place I'd ever felt totally happy, and I felt that I would never have to leave again. I was wrong.

Through the summer, to supplement our meager income, Alice and I grew a small truck garden, selling the vegetables in town for a nickel a bunch. We made close to a thousand dollars that summer from sales made out of a small child's wagon. I also learned to trap bullfrogs, which I sold. In the few idle hours I could salvage, I again enjoyed the company of my cousins, Ralph, Alton and Max. But, as autumn drew near, I discovered that my stay in Idaho was to be as transitory as all the others.

Alice was twenty-seven years old. She had devoted her life to mother and me, and now she wanted a life of her own; she wanted to be free to marry and raise her own family. She couldn't as long as she had to be responsible for me. Once more, I'd have to go. My bags were packed and preparations made to send me somewhere else, this time to Toledo to live with Dad. No one wanted me—or could afford to keep me—in Idaho, and I knew it. It made me feel bad, but I took it without whimpering. The years of rejection had stirred a fierce determination to someday be somebody, to be accepted and respected and wanted.

Thus far life had been that of an unwanted child—a "hand-me-down"—always, it seemed, being sent to live in yet another strange place, with people who probably didn't really want me, who probably didn't really care about me. By the time I was thirteen years old I'd had to pick up and move on six times.

I arrived in Toledo in late summer of 1930, alone, as always, dumped on a father I wasn't sure would want to keep me any longer than the other relatives with whom I'd been warehoused.

From my first day in Toledo, my driving ambition was to get back to Idaho. I'd loved the freedom of the West, the wide stretches of open fields where I could run, the quiet mountain streams where I could fish, and the deep forests where I could be alone with my dreams of someday being loved and wanted.

It was as if a two-thousand-mile cord connected me to the sunny mountains and the wind-kissed fields, a cord that tugged at me like a leash, urging me to return. I didn't like the city, and I didn't feel comfortable with father's new wife and family.

Our house was in the near-downtown section of Toledo. It was a bright and comfortable middle-class home in a neat middle-class neighborhood. Unlike so many millions of people in the 1930s, we were not suffering from the nation's economic woes; Dad had started a commercial window-washing business and had contracts with a number of the large department stores and office buildings in the downtown business district. We lived quite comfortably.

Dad's new wife was, like the home she kept, very pleasant; she always treated me with warmth and concern. But from the beginning there was a gulf between us that I knew we would never span, would never truly want to close. Her children were all grown, and I never became very close to them. I spent as much time as possible out of the house, walking around town, strolling along the Maumee River, sitting in the park.

At about this time I discovered the YMCA and the facilities they provided. During one of my first visits to the Y I learned of their wrestling programs and began to participate. There was something very therapeutic about grappling with another boy, using my strength to overcome his challenge. It seemed to eliminate some of the frustrations I was feeling. One of the coaches indicated that I had a natural talent for this very physical sport and began encouraging me to enter local competition. I did, and the next spring I won the city championship in the 125-pound class. Wrestling would continue to be my favorite sport until I was into my thirties.

During one of my wanderings around the city, I stopped at the railroad yards in South Toledo. There were an awful lot of trains moving in and out of the city and I discovered, talking to one of the yard workers, that Toledo was a major hub for east–west rail traffic. Suddenly I recalled something I'd seen on the train ride from Idaho. All along the route were well-populated encampments. A conductor had told me they were "hobo jungles," a stopping-off place for vagabonds who stole rides on trains. In these camps at trackside I had observed stoic-looking men seated around cook fires. And more than once I'd seen men in boxcars, a lot of them. It was apparent that a great many were riding the freight trains. I thought if I could learn to ride them maybe I could get back to Idaho when school was out for the summer. I studied railroad routes and hung around the freight yards, trying to make friends with railroad people.

Then, in a series of cheerless camps near the yards along the Maumee River, I discovered a collection of men without roots, men like those I'd seen along the tracks during the trip to Toledo. Although I wasn't aware of it at the time, my life was to become permanently bound to theirs.

CHAPTER 2

WAS IT HOE-BOY OR HI-BO?

The hobo was the outgrowth of two dramatic historical events: the construction of the first transcontinental railroads, and the American Civil War.

Just prior to the outbreak of the war between the states, the railroads began a period of tremendous growth that, shortly after the 1860s, would see the main lines span the continent from East to West with extensions of branches from the Deep South, to the fertile plains and the lush valleys of the far West. In 1850 there were approximately 9,000 miles of track in the continental United States. By the turn of the century there were more than 200,000 miles of rail line and the mileage was still growing.

This rapid growth required huge resources of common labor; armies of men fanned out to all reaches of the country, laying railroad track that would bring life-saving commerce and comfortable, affordable travel opportunities to even the tiniest settlements.

The men who built the railroads continued to use them as their favorite means of transportation even long after they left the employment rolls, catching a ride to another area looking for other work or just to see a different part of the country. In the early days, the railroads offered only minimal resistance to the relatively few men who chose to ride the freights. The riders were little trouble and the loss to the lines of passenger revenue was of little consequence since the railroads reasoned that anyone who would suffer the discomforts of drafty, sooty and bumpy boxcars were almost certainly those with no money to pay for the pleasant experience of riding inside where it was clean, warm and cheerful, and those who, if they couldn't ride free, would doubtlessly find some other means of moving from place to place.

But this charitable outlook on the part of the railroad barons changed with the tremendous influx of free riders immediately after the Civil War. Many of the veterans of the war had lost their homes, their families and their worldly possessions. Their lives had been terribly changed and thousands of them began wandering, looking in other parts of the nation for a new life, a future. They were, by virtue of their military experiences, well-trained for the nomadic life they had to live. They were used to living outdoors, were competent at foraging for food, knew how to recognize the most nutritious natural foods. They were accustomed to danger, and were toughened to the rigors of wandering the countryside.

They frequently sought to ride the trains as nonpaying passengers and soon became a serious concern to the railroads. Not only did the corporations now covet the money the "free-loaders" were denying them; they also saw a developing safety problem connected with those who stole rides. In a ten-year period, from 1898 to 1908 —the first period during which accident statistics were compiled by the railroads—47,000 railroad trespassers were killed, and this was just the *known* figure. It is estimated that as many as twice the reported number died while riding, boarding or attempting to leave the trains. "Tramp graveyards" sprang up along the right-of-way where the nameless were unceremoniously interred.

Of course, not all of the wanderers rode the trains; some traveled strictly on foot, walking across the country. They became known as "tramps." Others discovered that travel by rail was quicker and less time consuming than walking. They became the "hobos."

The hobos formally banded together shortly after the Civil War, forming a loose confederation which became known as the Brotherhood of 'Bos, which was in effect the first veteran's organization. Their ranks swelled in the late 1890s and again following World War I; they multiplied once more during the Great Depression and again after World War II.

• • •

The origin of the term "hobo" has been a continuing matter of speculation and controversy. Linguists and etymologists have never been in full agreement as to how the word evolved.

However, the hobos taught me that some believed the word originated around 1889 and came from the wanderers who hung their "bindles" on the end of a hoe, or garden implement, which they brought with them to facilitate obtaining short-term employment on farms or residences. They were called "hoe-boys," men who carried hoes. The term, they insist, was insulting to these men, who bristled at being called "boys." They began calling themselves "hoe-'bos." The term eventually became shortened to "ho-bo" and finally to "hobo."

Still others claimed that the term was the outgrowth of the salutation, "hi, boy." Again, so the stories go, many disliked being referred to as "boys," and encouraged the use of " 'bo," which they took to mean a man. This resulted in "hi, 'bo," which ultimately grew into "hobo."

Whatever the origin of the term, hobos themselves came to accept the term as a badge of honor as impressive as a graduate degree from a respected college or university, something that had been studied for and earned over a long period of time and after much hard work. They strove to make the title one that carried with it a high degree of pride.

Along with his few simple possessions the hobo also carried a "road name," an often colorful alias that identified him as a professional 'bo and sometimes gave clues to where he had come from, such as Louisiana Blue, New Orleans Slim, Cleveland Mushy and Philadelphia Shorty. Sometimes the name said something about a past occupation or activity: Sailor Bill, Hard Rock Kid, The Human Fly, Johnny Reb and Bank Job Ben.

Hobo lore has it that the first road names were adopted by a pair of former Union soldiers who called themselves "Erie Crip" and "Philly Pop." The practice of taking a road name was sometimes from a desire for anonymity and privacy and sometimes from a necessity to lessen the chance of being identified.

Hoboing reached a peak in the late-nineteenth century. The depression of 1893, caused by increasing industrialization, put hundreds of thousands out of work and sent them on the road searching for survival. In March 1893, a group formed by Jacob S. Coxey moved on Washington, D.C., from every part of the country. Coxey's Army—as it became known—sought to petition the government for assistance. Many had been forced to resort to almshouses for food and shelter.

By 1876, Pennsylvania had passed the first of the vagrancy statutes—"tramp laws"—that imposed criminal penalties on those who had no home, no job and no business wandering the countryside. This method of controlling the mass movement of the jobless soon spread into other states. Meanwhile, workhouses, penitentiaries and houses of correction were receiving a steady influx of what was soon seen as a ready source of cheap labor, and the practice of selling inmates into servitude became common. In some areas, men could be sentenced to chain gangs for as much as a year for no other offense than being without funds and no visible means of support.

In addition to growing community disapproval of the vagabond and the ever-increasing numbers on the road in the years following the economic depression of 1898, the railroads instituted severe measures to discourage the free use of its trains by establishing their own police units. Known as "bulls" or "railroad dicks," these frequently undisciplined thugs employed the most brutal methods to prevent unauthorized passengers from using the trains. The traveler soon came to know the wrath of the bull when caught on his train and began circulating warnings to others about the areas where the most dangerous bulls operated.

In the earliest days of "freight hopping," the most common places to ride were on top of the boxcars or in the open gondolas. Some engaged in the summertime practice of slipping through the roof hatch of a refrigerated car to ride in cool comfort. This was an extremely dangerous activity since a train crew member might accidentally —or intentionally—slip a locking pin through the hatch fastener, trapping the rider inside. Many were found frozen stiff when the car reached its destination.

And there were those who, for some unexplainable reason, opted for the highly perilous and most uncomfortable ride on the "cow catcher," a large plow-shaped device at the very front of the locomotive whose purpose was, as the name implies, to scoop errant livestock from the rails before they were ground beneath the wheels or caused a derailment. Another very life-threatening place to ride free was on the "rods" of a passenger car. Riding the rods required that the rider crawl up on the narrow brake rods that stretched just above the car's trucks—the four-wheel unit at the front and rear of each car. Perched there, the rider was in constant danger of losing his balance and falling under the wheels just inches below.

Yet another spot frequently used to ride the passenger cars was inside an empty battery box slung at the bottom of the car. The rider was in peril of being thrown out of the container and under the wheels when the car took a sudden or sharp turn.

• • •

By the early 1900s, several attempts were made to organize the vagabonds. The first and most notable was by the International Workers of the World. The IWW, with its headquarters in Chicago, Illinois, was established in July 1905. Because it was an extremely radical group whose avowed purpose was to replace the idea of "a fair day's pay for a fair day's work" (the hobo's creed) with the abolition of capitalism and the wage system, it appealed only to the most radical hobos.

IWW members were known as "Wobblies," and membership was gained by purchasing a "red card" which cost a dollar. Organizers for the IWW visited harvest fields and lumber and construction camps circulating rumors that no one would be permitted to work unless he had a red card, and that employers would refuse to hire or would greatly cut wages of nonmembers. Gangs of organizers frequently boarded freight trains and threw off those who couldn't produce a red card.

Also in 1905, there appeared the International Brotherhood Welfare Association. Strictly a hobo organization, the IBWA was the creation of the son of a wealthy St. Louis, Missouri, family named James Eads How. Disenchanted with the life of a rich man, How began wandering the country, got to know many hobos, and decided to try to improve their lives. His idea was to organize hobo migratory workers to enable them to have medical and legal aid, higher wages and better working conditions. The IBWA charter also promised to educate the public about the "rights of collective ownership in production and distribution," and to ". . . bring about the scientific, industrial, intellectual, moral and spiritual development of the masses." Because the organization appeared to be too close to the IWW and Communism, it ultimately failed.

In 1908, a young Ohioan, Jeff Davis, formed Hobos of America, Inc. Headquartered in Cincinnati with thirty-two members, Davis's group became one of the better known of the hobo organizations. Davis published his own newspaper, *Hobo News Review*, and opened several establishments called "Hotel de Gink" which were to provide shelter and food for hobos only; the idea and the places died after a few years.

In 1899, a number of businessmen in Britt, Iowa, heard of a small group of hobos who had formed a club known as "Tourists Union No. 63." The organization published a newspaper called the *Tourists Union Journal* and had already held three small conventions.

The Britt businessmen invited the Tourists Union to hold their 1900 convention in their tiny town and they promoted the event so well that the hobos were almost totally won over to the town. However, the Tourists Union did not return to Britt for more than thirty years. Then, in 1933, town leaders decided to try and resurrect the hobo celebration and to establish it as an annual event. Other small groups of organized hobos, many with self-proclaimed "kings," began attending and the "National Hobo Convention" has been held in Britt every year since 1933.

• • •

The Great Depression of the 1930s left millions of men unemployed and thousands homeless. Hungry, desperate men were traveling the country, staying in trackside camps, looking for any kind of work. They were the "transients," men vainly wandering from coast to coast, happily grabbing at the flimsiest rumor that someone was hiring in the next town or the next state.

Also in the camps were "bums" and "winos," sad-faced men for whom all hope had been exhausted, whose roads all led downward, and whose daily desire was for a panhandled half dollar to buy a meal or perhaps a warm bed for the bum, a drink or two of booze for the wino.

The "hobos," a strange group, difficult to understand, were among those found in the trackside jungles. They lived a quiet existence—were not rowdy and undisciplined, as the bums and winos often were. They didn't beg for money on street corners; they called at homes, offering to chop wood or do other chores in exchange for a meal. They actively avoided the others, establishing their circle apart from the bums, winos and transients. Their camps were always neat, free of trash and litter.

Their manner of dress also identified them. Usually they wore black or dark blue suits of a good quality, often a white shirt and a neckerchief and many times a necktie. They selected dark clothing to make it more difficult to be seen by railroad police at night, and the suit, shirt and tie gave them a more presentable appearance when they called at residences asking for work. They never wore flashy clothes; they didn't sport suntans or work clothes; nor did they wear overalls, which they considered "farmerish."

I discovered that hobos were a fastidious lot; their camps were most often established by a river or a stream next to a rail line to provide water to wash, or "boil up," their clothes.

The two other groups of vagrants—the "bums" and the "winos"—were usually shiftless and lazy. They moved about more nomadically than did the tramps and the hobos, who tended to have fairly well-defined "circuits" that they would cover during the year.

Many hobos and tramps were former professional men, craftsmen, printers and construction workers who periodically offered their services in exchange for room and board and a little pocket money before moving on. Tramp printers and typesetters were well known to newspapermen into the 1940s; tramp bricklayers and cement workers and construction "boomers" exist to some degree to this day. These men were frequently tops in their fields—they had to be, in order to get work when they wanted it—and often came from both hobo and tramp groups.

Hobos and tramps loathed being referred to as "bums." They also chafed under the name "wino." They believed themselves to be more honorable, more ethical, more honest and more worthwhile than the bum or the wino, whom they considered worthless, selfish and dishonest.

The thing that set the hobo and the tramp dramatically apart from the bum, the wino and the transient was the fact that the hobo and the tramp lived their unorthodox life-style out of pure choice. They were not driven to it out of economic desperation as were the transients—and to some extent, the bums. And while they were not necessarily abstainers, the hobos and tramps were not emotionally or physically tied to and rendered helpless by an addiction to alcohol, as were the winos.

The hobo was what he was because that was what he wanted to be. It was his calling, his profession, his reason for being.

I was intrigued by this gentle, courteous vagabond group. But, in the beginning, while they were always polite to me, they seemed uncomfortable and suspicious when I remained in camp more than a few minutes; to them kids in camp spelled trouble, and they wouldn't allow them to hang around. I would learn later why they felt this way.

However, I discovered that if I brought some potatoes or onions to give them they would let me sit by the fire and listen to their conversations . . . for a little while, at least.

Soon I was bringing canned food along with the vegetables when I went down to the camp. In exchange, I was permitted to stay longer and was made to feel welcome. They began educating me in the history of hoboing, a subject that totally enthralled me, and they called me "Idaho," because I had just come from there. I'd sit for hours listening to every word. Some of these men were in their seventies and even their eighties and knew exactly how hoboing had begun and told wonderful stories about some of the famous 'bos.

I was impressed by the high standards the hobos set for themselves and I longed to be accepted by this elite group. Throughout the winter of 1930–31, I spent as much time as possible with the hobos in Toledo, sitting around the fires outside their cardboard shelters, listening to their stories, learning their history and their philosophy of life. Although, at this time, I had no plans to dedicate my life to hoboing, I felt I could benefit from their experience, that I might learn how to travel to Idaho, to survive the trip and to return safely when school reopened in the fall.

In the spring of 1931, I announced to my hobo friends that I was going on the road, back to Idaho. The hobos tried to discourage me. They told me of the "road kids," youngsters like myself, who ran away from home and tried to ride the freights. A lot of bad things happened to them, and a lot of them got killed.

"I can take care of myself. I can whip a man, and nobody's gonna bother me," I told them.

"You'll get killed, boy, it's too dangerous," they insisted.

But I would not be convinced.

"I can get by and I'm gonna go."

Realizing that I was determined, the hobos relented.

"We'd better teach this kid or he'll get himself killed the first day."

They began with safety rules: how to move around a freight yard and not get run over; they cautioned me never to crawl under a boxcar, moving or not, and they taught me the safe way to board a rolling freight car, how to swing up on a boxcar ladder, which hand to use and how to grip the rungs, which foot to use to avoid swinging between the cars and losing the handhold. They taught me to blouse my pant legs—using a rubber band, a piece of string or rope or a bicycle clip—to keep my trousers from catching on something and throwing me under the wheels; how to move between cars, avoiding the couplings that could grab the heels of the careless and pinch part of a foot off. They taught me how to get off a moving car, how to test the speed to be certain the car wasn't rolling too fast.

The hobos taught me the courtesy and respect I had to show others, particularly to railroad men, to housewives and to men I would have to approach to ask for a meal. They taught me how to inquire of men in the freight yards—brakemen and switchmen and train crews—which freights were leaving and where they were headed.

"If you're polite and say, 'yes sir, no sir, please sir,' most railroad men will help you," they told me.

I learned that there was a mutual respect held by hobos and railroad men; the railroad people knew that the hobo would never steal, no matter how hungry, no matter how desperate. He would never break into a boxcar. The hobo, in turn, believed that he owed the railroad that honesty in exchange for the opportunity to travel on the freights. Riding as an unpaid passenger was not allowed . . . supposedly. The hobo knew it, the railroad men knew it. But it went on, largely with the tacit approval and assistance of the men in the yards.

The railroad police—the "bulls"—were a different matter. It was their job to keep all unauthorized passengers off the trains and all trespassers off railroad property, and many sadistically enjoyed what they did. Many were former city and state police who had been dismissed for brutality, and some railroads actively sought them out because they were already trained policemen and were just naturally mean as hell.

The hobo recognized the bull as their most dangerous

enemy, a manhunter who had been given a license to kill . . . and, at times, did.

One night, in the Toledo freight yards, I witnessed how brutally effective the bulls could be. A bum had apparently broken into a boxcar loaded with chickens, or possibly beef, when a railroad policeman came upon him. I was standing in the shadow of a nearby boxcar and saw the bull grab the bum and begin flailing at the hapless man with a club. He beat him unconscious and then kicked him in the ribs and stomach. I flattened myself against the car and held my breath; I was certain my thundering heart would be heard by the savage railroad cop. It seemed that he kept beating the man for hours, but it probably lasted only two or three minutes. The unfortunate victim finally lay motionless, with only a kind of grunting sound coming from him whenever the bull kicked him in the chest or stomach. From the bull I could hear a low, mean growl that lasted throughout the beating, the audible insanity of a man out of control.

At last, the cop, panting for breath, stopped pounding, grabbed the unconscious bum by the back of his collar and dragged him away, the beads of sweat on his face glistening in the low illumination of a nearby yard light. He passed within five feet of me, but his head was turned away, looking down at the still figure he was hauling away with him. I never found out what happened to the bum, how seriously injured he'd been or whether he survived the vicious beating the railroad bull had given him. However, I did see the policeman again. One afternoon as I was headed for the hobo jungle, I spotted him standing in the rail yard talking to a workman, smiling pleasantly and laughing. He looked just like anyone else and I remember thinking that his face looked soft and friendly and that if I'd met him on the street I probably would have thought he was a kind and gentle man. Several years later I learned that he had been murdered in a rail yard down near Lima, Ohio, by a bum he had beaten several months earlier. The bum had paid a kid to tell the cop that he'd seen someone sleeping in an open freight car. When the bull approached, the bum raised up and shot him in the face, killing him instantly. They never caught the bum.

The shocking, sickening beating I had witnessed left me shaken; I had never seen so vivid an example of one man's violence against another, and the grisly vision and the terrible sounds of the club against flesh and the boot against bone and the pitiful cries and groans of the helpless victim filled my restless sleep during many dark and fearful nights that followed.

There would be instances in the days to come when I would observe even greater brutality and would, myself, be the victim of such attacks.

My hobo training included signals hobos left for other 'bos, a branch bent at a strange angle and fastened there with a rubber band or a piece of string, chalked messages on fences or walls or water tanks, signs that indicated the houses and businesses that were "easy touches" for a meal or a day's work.

I was taught how to identify myself to other hobos and how to conduct myself when in their jungles, to explain that I was not a bum or a wino or a road kid. They taught me what clothing and necessities to take with me and how to pack them in a bedroll or "bindle."

Attempting such a long and complex journey without the expert advice and counsel the hobos provided me would have been, at best, dangerous, at worst, catastrophic. In my zeal to return to Idaho, I would doubtlessly have embarked on the ill-advised trek. Whether or not I would have arrived safely can only be a matter of conjecture. Surely, the assistance generously given by the quiet group of hobos lessened the chances of serious consequences for me.

The names and faces of these caring men have drifted behind the curtain of more than fifty years. But the memory of what they did for me and what they taught me has remained a vivid, invaluable education, one I could never forget.

. . .

I had announced to several school chums that I was intending to ride the freights to Idaho. To most it was idle boasting, but among those who knew me best, one believed what I had said. His name was Red McVicker and he was about as unhappy with his home life as I was with mine.

"You're really goin', ain't you, Maury?"

"Yep, I'm goin' soon as school's out," I told him.

"Take me with you; I really want to go with you."

"You don't know anything about riding freights."

"Neither do you; you ain't never rode one before."

"Yeah, but the hobos taught me what to do and how to conduct myself."

"Then, teach me!"

It was obvious that Red was determined to leave home, and I realized that having a traveling companion would be more enjoyable and it would be safer.

As the warm, gentle breezes of early June began pushing north of the Ohio River Valley, Red and I were excitedly completing plans for our departure.

Without realizing it, I was about to embark on the most fateful journey of my young life, and I would never be the same because of it. A juvenile desire to try and recapture a more pleasant time would prod me into travels that would fill a lifetime, thrilling adventures which would make my life satisfying and complete. The iron road would become a seductive mistress for me, one whose tender caress would continuously call me back over the span of a third of a century.

CHAPTER 3

MY FIRST ADVENTURE

On a pleasant sunny day in mid-June 1931, classes at Toledo's Jones Junior High School were dismissed for the summer.

For most students it meant a lazy vacation of swimming in the Maumee River or nearby Lake Erie or picnicing or sleeping late in the morning or just "hangin' around." For me and my friend Red McVicker, it meant much more.

I never knew Red's actual first name: everyone called him "Red," even the teachers. He was a naive sort, had never been far from home. He didn't have the fortitude for the hard life we would face, and taking him along might have proved to be an unfortunate decision. But on that warm spring day, Red and I were thinking only of the great adventure we were beginning.

As soon as I could get away from school, I dashed home to pack my bindle, a piece of coarse canvas into which I rolled a blanket, a couple of clean shirts, underwear, socks, an extra pair of work pants and a tooth brush. In years to come I would adopt the more "formal" hobo attire of a dark suit and a white shirt, but for now I was restricted by economic considerations to the suntans that were the usual kids' street clothes.

I'd said nothing to my father concerning my plans to ride the freights back to Idaho for the summer; I planned to write him when I arrived to let him know I was safe. The only mention I made about leaving Toledo was to my stepmother.

"I'm gettin' out of here," I said as I was walking out the back door. "I'll be back in the fall."

She made no attempt to stop me. She understood—perhaps better than anyone—that there were some things I just had to do. I didn't feel guilty about leaving without talking it over with Dad; as a matter of fact, the idea never occurred to me. And I didn't look upon leaving as "running away from home." I was just doing what I had to do, going back to Idaho. Through the long winter my concentration had been fixed on leaving as soon as school was out. There simply wasn't time to consider alternatives to heading west or to discuss my plans with my father, who certainly would have vetoed the unreasonably dangerous trip. Nor did the thought occur to me that Dad would worry about me. I was so confident that I could make the journey safely, there was no room for the possibility that others might assume that I couldn't.

This would be my initiation into the "brotherhood," and the lessons I was to learn during these first few months would color and shade my life for decades to come. I was taking the first steps that would lead me along a noble pathway, toward a time when I would be not just a wanderer but King of the Hobos.

• • •

Red and I met on the outskirts of the freight yards, waiting in a small patch of woods until the sun was setting before moving into the yards to look for a departing train. Toledo was on the east–west main line between the Atlantic coast ports and Chicago; all we needed to do was catch any train headed west and we would be on our way to Chicago.

With our bindles slung over our shoulders, McVicker and I benignly strolled into the freight yard, thus violating one of the cardinal rules the hobos had taught me. We were supposed to lay in the weeds until the train started moving. Instead, we just walked in, looking around, like we owned the place. A brakeman caught us. Seeing how young we were and assuming that we were running away from home, he attempted to discourage our plans.

"You little bastards," he shouted, "get out of these yards and don't you ever come back around these freight trains."

Then, to impress his order upon us, he assisted us off the property with well-placed and very painful kicks to our backsides. He kicked me just once, but so hard that it hurt for a long time, and I thought that nobody else was ever going to kick me like that again because they weren't going to catch me again . . . ever.

We sailed out of the yards like our pants were on fire, whining and whimpering all the way. We dashed back to the wooded area near the yards to nurse our aching posteriors and to decide what we should do next.

"Well, I guess that's it, we'll never get a train now," Red moaned.

"The hell we won't," I spat back. "What happened with that brakeman ain't gonna change my mind one bit. We'll just wait for the right opportunity."

We'd been hiding in the woods for perhaps an hour when I spied a long, westbound freight moving toward the main line. I could see several open, empty boxcars. "There's our chance," I said, grabbing my bindle and moving out of the woods, with Red close on my heels. We dashed back into the yard, got alongside the train as it was picking up speed and hauled ourselves into the car.

The exhilaration of chasing and catching the train—our very first—left us panting on the floor of the car as it moved out of Toledo heading for Elkhart, Indiana, 120 miles west.

"We done it," Red shouted, laughing. "By God, Maury, we actually done it!"

As the train sped through the darkness, I sat, watching the flat countryside pass the open boxcar door. The soot and smoke and cinders swirled around the inside of the car, the acrid smell filled my nostrils, the low throaty moan of the engine's whistle echoed around me, the groan of the twisting wood and steel of the boxcar mixed with the rumble of the wheels on the rails, creating a thundering racket that was sweet music to my happy ears.

It had been an exciting experience and I looked forward to the long trip ahead. It had been frightening, too—the danger involved in catching the moving train, and the pain at the hands of the brakeman that left my hip and buttocks throbbing, all combined to cause my heart to race excitedly. Now, in the quiet of the blackened car, I tingled with thoughts of what the future held.

About two hours after boarding, the train began to slow. Looking out the door I could see the lights of a large rail yard.

"We're comin' into Elkhart."

In the yards, the train moved back and forth, dropping cars and hooking on to others. Red and I stayed huddled in a darkened corner of the boxcar, waiting for the train to move back on the main line. Occasionally, a yard workman or a bull peeked inside, but we weren't spotted hiding in the shadows. Finally, after about an hour, the train began to move, slowly picking up speed as it chugged out of the yards. We breathed a heavy sigh of relief. Then came a commotion alongside the car. A head and shoulders appeared at the ledge beneath the door and then the body of a man, clambering up into the car, then another, then another. Three men had joined us.

"Hi, there, fellas," one of them said, looking us over carefully.

He was not a hobo; his clothes told me that. Nor were the other two, who said nothing as they moved to the opposite end of the car and hunkered down on the floor.

"You boys goin' to Chicago?" The first asked.

I nodded and grunted in the affirmative. I wasn't frightened of this man. But neither was I anxious to engage him in lengthy conversation. My hobo mentors had been very explicit in their warnings that I should not become too chummy with anyone I hadn't had a chance to observe carefully for a time.

When I failed to respond enthusiastically to his questions, the man shrugged, walked to the end of the car and joined the others. They sat together throughout the trip, talking quietly among themselves.

It was still dark as the freight slid along the rails and over switches into the New York Central yards in south Chicago, part of the largest railroad center in the world.

Our major problem at that point was obtaining food; neither of us had money, we'd left home without a cent, and we hadn't eaten in almost twenty hours.

We left the train near the Union Stockyards, five miles south of the Chicago Loop, and began searching for a place we might get a meal. The streets were crowded with men and women who had started out before dawn looking for jobs—of any kind. They trudged sullenly past shops and factories ornamented with signs proclaiming: "No Help Wanted." They joined long lines without knowing exactly where the line was going or what the line was for, grasping at every chance that their luck might change, that they might capture one of the rare offers of employment they'd heard about from men on street corners and smoky saloons.

Oddly enough, in the midst of the catastrophic Depression, there *were* jobs, and within a few hours a pair of teenaged boys, strangers in this big city, each got one. Red and I went into a small diner near the stockyards, walked up to the counter and waited for the man at the grill to notice us.

"What can I do for you, fellas?" he asked in a friendly voice that gave me added courage.

"Mister, me and my partner are lookin' for some work to do to earn a meal. Can we wash dishes or mop some floors or something like that?"

He smiled and looked us over.

"You're not from around here, are you?"

"No, sir."

"Where're you from?"

"Toledo, sir . . . Ohio, sir."

"Runaways?"

"No, sir. We're headin' out to Idaho where my mother lives."

He paused and thought for a moment.

"Sure, I can always use dishwashers. If you do a good job, I'll feed you. You want to work the whole day?"

"Sure do," I replied enthusiastically.

In those days there were always places that needed dishwashers and floor moppers. All the dishes were done by hand and restaurants were constantly short of personnel to do these menial jobs, especially someone to do the pots and pans. The jobs were sporadic and the pay was notoriously low; only the most desperate were happy to have them.

We worked a full twelve hours doing the dishes, the pots and pans, cleaning the counters and the tables, sweeping and mopping the floors, emptying the garbage and any other small tasks the manager could find for us. In exchange, we were given a breakfast of ham and eggs and milk, a lunch of soup, a sandwich and iced tea, and a dinner of chili and crackers and coffee with canned milk.

"You did a good job, fellas," the manager said at the

end of the day. "I could use you again tomorrow, if you're interested."

The chance to insure full bellies was set against the unattractive geographic area in which we were working. The restaurant was down by the stockyards and the odor in the air was terrible. But, more than the smell, it was a very tough place back then, and I was anxious to get out as quick as I could.

"If we worked tomorrow, could we also get some food to take with us?"

The manager laughed: "Well, now, that will depend on how much food you want."

"I'm talkin' some sandwiches to eat on the train; maybe three or four apiece."

"You're quite a horse trader, ain't you? It's a deal, but you'll have to work plenty hard."

We agreed and left to find a place to sleep. I had noticed cattle barns near the edge of the rail yards and, recalling what the Toledo hobos had told me, led Red to the barns. Inside we found high stacks of hay, a safe and comfortable place to bed down for the night. On future trips, I would discover that these cattle barns afforded an excellent place to pick up a little money cleaning cattle pens and doing other chores. And there was always running water available to wash or to quench one's thirst.

We were at the diner at six thirty the following morning. The manager gave us each a bowl of hot oatmeal and milk and we went to work.

About seven that evening, with a sack of sandwiches—and a dime the manager had given us to take a streetcar—we headed across town for the Blue Island yards where, I had learned, the trains going west were made up. It was my plan to ride the Rock Island Line as far as Omaha, Nebraska, and then catch the freights of the Union Pacific that serviced the northern tier of states, including Idaho.

While Red remained outside, I moved cautiously into the yards where I spotted a workman. Carefully walking up to him, I said politely, "Sir, I'm looking to head on out of here, out west. Could you tell me which trains might be headed for Omaha?"

The man eyed me suspiciously, branding me as a "road kid." He was at first reluctant to help this boy who he felt should be turned over to the police and sent back home. But I guess I had been so respectful, the workman gave in.

"Well, there's one making up for a nine o'clock call over on track ten. You'll see the string over there with the caboose hooked on."

I thanked him profusely and hurried back to where Red was waiting to tell him what the workman had said.

"When we see the engine hook on, that's when we make our play."

In the meantime we scouted around and found track ten and studied the string of cars, finding several with open doors. As the locomotive backed in to connect to the train, we crept carefully into the yards and headed for the open cars, keeping a watchful eye for railroad police. Selecting one of the boxcars, we crawled on board and huddled in the darkened corner waiting for the train to pick up speed and move out to the main line.

"Remember," the hobos in Toledo had warned me, "don't go poking your head out of the car while the train is still in the yards. Keep back and don't move."

Soon, the train was speeding along the tracks at fifty or sixty miles an hour and we were once again underway. The trip was largely uneventful. The train we were riding turned out to be a local, stopping at every town along the route between Chicago and Omaha. Other travelers climbed on at various stops; for the most part they were silent and self-contained, deep in their own private thoughts, and I didn't feel threatened or ill at ease with them.

When cars were to be dropped off and other cars added, the unauthorized passengers had as much as two or even three hours to leave the train while the switching was being done. The following morning, just before we got to Omaha, the others went out hustling for food and I decided Red and I should do the same; the supply of sandwiches we'd brought with us had been eaten during the night.

It was hard to get something to eat because there were so many men riding the trains. Everything within a mile or two of the tracks was "bummed" to death. Anyone who lived within a half mile of the yards had somebody knocking at the back door every half hour. I soon became accustomed to hearing a beleaguered housewife explaining, "We don't hardly have enough for ourselves."

Fortunately, our youth worked in our favor on this trip, frequently allowing us to obtain work and meals where older men couldn't. Several times I went to houses where two or three guys ahead of me had been refused food and I got fed.

During the first few days of our trip begging for food—even in exchange for work—was difficult for me. I hated to go to a door and try to get something to eat; I was very bashful about that. But Red was even worse; he was scared to death to go to a door and ask for a meal. For quite a while I had to get enough for both of us.

Aside from the embarrassment, approaching a house to offer work in exchange for a meal was not without its potential dangers. The Toledo hobos had cautioned me to observe very strict rules in attempting to obtain a meal from a housewife.

"*Never* go inside the house, even if the housewife invites you in," I was told. "You can't be sure that her husband won't come home unexpected and figure you're up to no good."

I was told that if food was offered, I should always ask the woman to hand it out the door to me.

The caution had developed over many years of unfortunate consequences for careless hobos; the request that the offering be handed out became a common practice among the true hobos and resulted in the term "hand out."

I had prepared a formal speech for my first attempt at "backdoor bumming," and I rehearsed it as I walked up to a house on the outskirts of Omaha: "Lady, would you have any work I could do to earn something to eat?"

I knocked on the door, mentally going over the speech one more time. Suddenly the door opened and I was faced with an extremely pretty girl about my age, standing there smiling sweetly. I could only stand there looking at her, stuttering and stammering; I thought she was so lovely, I couldn't say what I wanted. Finally, in desperation, I was able to blurt out:

"Girl, could you give me a drink of water? I'm thirsty."

It took two or three hours before I had mustered the courage to try again. This time I was met by a much older woman, was able to recite my little speech and was rewarded with something to eat. From then on I did all right; I wasn't bashful anymore.

Our first stop at a hobo jungle also proved to be a challenge.

As it had been in Toledo, when I first attempted to enter the hobos' camp there, I found a strong resentment and suspicion when Red and I walked into our first hobo camp, near North Platte, Nebraska.

Bums, as I was to discover later, often had kids in their camps. Known as "punks," the teenagers were veritable slaves, forced to hustle food and money for their "masters," and frequently beaten and abused sexually. They were a ragged, seedy-looking bunch with sad, frightened eyes embedded in hard, unhappy faces. I found it incredible that these boys, my own age and sometimes several years older, could allow themselves to be used in such a degrading and disgusting fashion. They must have come from homes far more unhappy than mine, or perhaps from no homes at all.

The hobos, fearing they would be accused of this kind

of perversion, discouraged the young from entering their circle. They segregated themselves from the other vagabonds, setting up their camps farther down river.

The North Platte jungle was a fairly large camp, with perhaps fifty or sixty men sitting around a dozen fires. I could tell by looking at them and the area of the first circles we came to that they weren't hobos; they were too dirty. We went on down the river a short distance and found the hobo camp.

I strolled up to the first hobo fire, ready to introduce myself when one of the men said curtly:

"Get along, punk, we don't want no trouble around here."

"I'm no 'punk' and don't call me that unless you want to fight me," I bristled.

The image of a fearlessly determined 125-pound teenager, willing to take on anyone in camp, at first astonished the hobos sitting there. They looked at me for a long moment, and then the 'bo who had insulted me burst into laughter and the others joined in.

"Well, I'll be damned. I really think you would fight us," the first 'bo said, tears of humor beginning to flow on his cheeks.

I apologized for being sassy and courteously introduced myself, explaining that my partner and I were traveling to Idaho and that I had hobo friends in Toledo. I mentioned the names of the hobos there and, fortunately, they knew some of them, which helped a great deal.

After the introduction, I stood and waited to see if we'd be invited to sit down. The men looked at one another, and each nodded, signaling his willingness to have us join them and share the food that was in the cooking pot.

There were very strict rules of etiquette which I knew must be observed when in a hobo jungle. You might find four or five cook fires in a jungle with five or six men sitting around each one. The procedure was to walk up to the first and introduce yourself or make some pleasantry. But if they didn't invite you to join them, you excused yourself and walked on to the next. And if the next bunch didn't invite you, you went to the next fire and the next and the next. And if you received no invitations from any of the men in the jungle, you went on and built your own fire and cooked up whatever you had or could scrounge in town.

This ritual was not conducted out of a lack of hospitality or unkindness but rather from simple economics, both of words as well as deed. There might be six guys who had just prepared a pot with only enough food for six. They couldn't invite someone to sit down if there wasn't enough to share, so they just wouldn't. It wasn't an insult to the hobo who hadn't been invited; he would know that if there was enough to share, he would have been asked to sit down. Hobos traditionally shared their good fortune. But, if there was not enough in the pot, they didn't feel obliged to make excuses or explanations to a new arrival. They simply said nothing at all.

After a meal, the hobos congregated around a single large fire, and all were welcome to sit there. It was then that stories and songs and poems would be exchanged.

I was very impressed with the reading habits of the hobos. Most had no formal education, and yet they seemed among the best-read individuals I have ever known. They read everything they could get their hands on: books, magazines, newspapers, anything they found lying around. There was a saying that you could easily tell a hobo from a bum because, while they both lined their coats and jackets with insulating newspapers, the hobo *read* his first.

In every hobo jungle, tin cans, pots and pans were hung from the branches of trees, carefully cleaned and ready for any hobo to use to prepare his meal. When the 'bo left the camp, the utensils were as clean as when he had arrived and were carefully hung back among the branches. If there were no utensils in camp, the hobo would scrounge a few large tins and maybe a pot and pan or two from town. He would clean and polish them and leave them there for the hobos who would follow.

The area was always tidied up for the next occupants, the ground swept with willow branches to remove crumbs, other food that might attract bugs, and leaves and other debris. They followed the Indian custom of always leaving a campground the way they found it.

A short distance from camp, the hobo could often find handmade box traps that had been left set and frequently had live game inside that had been caught the night before, and was now waiting for the hobo's dinner. Hunting in the camps near rail yards was unlawful, thereby creating a natural game preserve that had an abundance of possum, woodchuck, raccoon and occasionally pheasant, drawn to the area by the grain littering the roadbed that had been spilled from passing freight trains.

The camps of the bums and winos were never as neat and clean as those of the hobos, which caused resentment between the groups because of the difference in lifestyles. Hobos attempted to avoid the others as much as possible because of their lack of ethics and cleanliness, while the bums and winos disdained the hobos for their "false sense of superiority."

The transients, on the other hand, tended to be a less well-defined group, often able to circulate within either of the divergent social bodies.

That first night in a hobo camp away from Toledo was a thrilling, satisfying experience for me. Even Red—who tended to view hobos with ridicule in spite of what I'd told him about them—thoroughly enjoyed the pleasant evening by the fire, listening to their stories and their poems and songs. I particularly savored the robust music they were able to produce from a harmonica (which they called a "mouth organ") and a Jew's harp, a small handheld metal instrument consisting of an oval frame and a thin metal strip fastened to the center of the frame, which was bent at the free end. By holding it between the lips and plucking or strumming on the metal strip, a delightful twangy sound would be produced that served as a rhythm section to the harmonica's melody. I later mastered this inexpensive musical instrument and enjoyed many happy evenings sitting in with hobo bands.

At each encampment we visited on that first trip I made new friends that I was able use as references at the next stop. And my hobo education continued as well. I was told which yards to avoid because of sadistic railroad bulls; which jungles along their route were the safest; and which towns were best for getting a meal and/or work. I was also warned of some of the special dangers to be found traveling in the West. One of the things I was told was not to ride the trains at night in the high country. Men had frozen to death in boxcars going over the Rockies, even in the summer.

With each new camp we visited, my appreciation for the hobos grew. Each evening I sat by the fire, listening to the stories the hobos exchanged, exciting stories, funny and beautiful and sad stories of their years on the road. I'd sit, with the flaming logs warming my face, until I couldn't keep my eyes open any longer, and then I would roll up in my blanket and continue to listen until I fell happily and soundly asleep.

I felt so very comfortable with these quiet men who had, it seemed to me, captured the secret of true happiness and satisfaction. Many of them could have been very successful in almost any profession—I learned later that a great many *had* been successful professionals before going on the road. Such men might have achieved great wealth, might have been highly respected and admired leaders of the community. But, for some reason I did not understand in the summer of 1931, they chose instead to find happiness wandering from place to place, owning nothing, owing nothing, responsible only to themselves, hurting no one, asking just to be let alone.

The trip from Chicago to Emmett, Idaho, lasted just over three days and took us through Grand Island and

North Platte, Nebraska; Cheyenne, Laramie and Green River, Wyoming; Pocatello, Boise and Caldwell, Idaho: a distance of 1,738 miles.

My mother and sister were surprised and delighted to see me when I arrived in Emmett, but I was chastised for taking such a risk to get back there. One of my first acts after arrival was to write a letter to my father, telling him where I was and promising to be back in Toledo in time for the fall semester of school. Then I took Red around to the farms and ranches in the area and secured summer jobs for both of us. We helped with the harvests and picked fruit.

It was a thoroughly happy time for me; I was back where I truly wanted to be, with my family and friends. But Red, unaccustomed to country living and the brutally hard work, tired quickly of the West.

With several weeks remaining before we would have to begin the return trip, Red announced that he wanted to leave for home immediately, and I agreed to return with him. But we hadn't gone far when I decided to take advantage of the extra travel time available to see more of the country. Red was not interested—he wanted to get back to Toledo as fast as possible. So we parted amicably, with Red retracing the route we had taken out and I heading south through Denver and Pueblo, Colorado. I worried about him the whole time back. He really wasn't cut out for traveling. I was extremely relieved when I learned that he had made it back safely. But he had vowed never to make such a trip again. And I was relieved about that, too!

I had new work clothes and almost a hundred dollars earned in the Idaho harvests, which I carried in a small leather pouch tied around my waist. In later years I found that the pouch, when packed with silver dollars, made an excellent blackjack with which to defend myself. I would have much use for such a weapon.

With each day of the trip back, I was growing more and

more confident, more self-assured. I continued to meet and be accepted by the hobos. I listened carefully and profited by the advice I was given. My youth continued to provide protection for me; I was rarely bothered by any of the dangerous elements among those traveling the country in those hard days; the police largely tended to ignore me and I could always find someone who would take pity on me and give me a meal.

The extended journey took me to El Paso, Fort Worth and Dallas, Texas; then to Nashville, Tennessee, and Louisville, Kentucky. On arrival in Louisville, I had another excruciating confrontation with the railroad police.

I had heard from other 'bos that there were some real bad bulls in the Louisville yards, very sadistic, so I wanted to get off the train before it got in the yard. Lowering myself on the freight car ladder as the train neared Louisville, I used a method the hobos had taught me to test the speed of the train. You can't always tell from just looking at the ground how fast the train is moving. If you jump when it's going too fast you can be seriously hurt, bones broken and cinders in your face. To determine if it's safe to jump, I was instructed to hang from the ladder rung and touch one foot on the ground. If it flies back up and kicks you in the seat, the train's going too fast to jump.

Coming into the yard, I had been periodically testing, but found that the speed was still too high to make the jump safely. Then, I looked up and saw this fella step out from behind parked boxcars ahead. He looked like a yard worker, with overalls and everything, but when I got closer, I saw him pull out a revolver and knew he was a railroad cop.

As I drew near, the policeman shouted for me to "get off, get off."

I yelled back, "can't get off, going too fast."

The policeman again ordered me to get off and as the car, with me clinging to the ladder, passed his position, he swung his pistol, striking a severe blow to my right thigh. It paralyzed my leg, making it impossible to get off just then.

The policeman then took aim and fired at me. The bullet hit the side of the boxcar next to my head, sending out a shower of wood splinters that embedded themselves in my arm. It felt like buckshot hitting me. Later, I had to take the splinters out with a pocket knife.

Having missed possible death by mere inches didn't register just then; the agony I felt in my leg occupied all my attention at that moment. Because of the blow to my leg, I had to wait until the train had completely stopped rolling at the far end of the yard and then hurriedly limp away before the bull could catch me. My injured leg hurt terribly for weeks afterward, and to this day I still carry a ping-pong-ball-sized knot on my leg from that confrontation with the Louisville bull.

Hurting but not discouraged, I painfully made my way to Cincinnati and then, with just a few days of summer recess remaining, to Toledo.

I had *done* it! I had gone on the road, traveling close to five thousand miles at a cost of a five-cent streetcar ride across Chicago.

I limped into the house, dropping my bindle on the floor.

My father would tell me years later that the first thing he noticed was that I had a quiet but unmistakable maturity that had not been present when I'd left in June. He looked at me with relief in his eyes but made no attempt to criticize me for my ill-considered wanderings. Instead, he simply asked why I had gone west, and I replied that I went to find work.

"You could have worked with me during the summer, you know."

Yes, I knew, but work was not all I had sought in the summer of 1931. I had gone looking for thrills, for excitement. I had gone searching for adventure. And I had found it.

But more than the thrills, the excitement and the adventure, I had gone looking for someone to belong to. I had always felt shut out, a cast-off, never really a member of a group or family. The kindly, soft-spoken hobos in Toledo and on the road had accepted me, had taken me into their private circle, made me feel welcome and one of them. Now I *really* belonged; I had a family.

I knew that I would go on the road again. In fact, I was already making plans for the next summer.

CHAPTER 4

TRAVELING ON ZERO DOLLARS A DAY

"Yeah, we heard about ya," the old hobo chuckled.

Almost as soon as I arrived back in Toledo I went down to the hobo jungle to let my friends know I had made the trip safely and to tell them of some of my adventures. But word of my travels had filtered in during the summer, carried by hobos who stopped in Toledo.

I thanked the men who had so carefully prepared me for my first trip on the iron road.

"I might not have survived the trip if I hadn't been taught so good," I told them.

I had learned a great deal during the summer, too, and now felt that I was fully equipped to travel anywhere at any time. The long, dreary winter seemed unending and distressingly bleak as I waited without patience to be on my way again.

As a means of relieving boredom I continued in the YMCA wrestling program, repeating the success I'd had the year before by winning my second city championship —this time in the 135-pound class. And I kept myself occupied working for my father as a window washer.

As the ice on the Maumee River began to break up and float toward Lake Erie, and the leaves on the maple, birch and willow trees appeared, and the winter browns turned to springtime greens, the itch to be on my way again became unbearable.

I was going back to Idaho; the mysteries of places as yet unseen would have to wait for one more year. While Red McVickers would not be accompanying me this year, I was not going alone. A classmate at Jones Junior High School, Jimmy Lester OdNeal had been enchanted by the stories Red and I brought back from our travels of the previous summer.

"Boy, I'd love to do that," he exclaimed each time he heard us talk of our summer on the road.

"Okay, if you want to go, I'll take you with me," I finally told him. "But, you'll have to learn the hobo rules and live by them."

J. L., as he was called, had spent most of his childhood on the farm, as I had. He was very strong and much more aggressive than McVickers, and I knew he'd be a perfect hoboing partner. We became close friends and would travel together for the next several years.

We left the day school was out for the summer. I'd told my father when I returned from my first trip that I'd be going again this summer, so he was prepared for my departure and didn't try to change my mind. J. L. also informed his family of our plans to ride the freights out to Idaho. His mother didn't really want him to leave, but there were twelve mouths to feed in his family and they were reduced to living on welfare during the Depression. So, letting him fend for himself for three months had certain advantages for the beleaguered OdNeals.

I decided that taking the same route to Idaho that Red

and I used the year before was the fastest and the easiest way to travel. Then, too, I was looking forward to visiting the familiar jungles and, perhaps, seeing some of the friends I'd met on my first trip.

I had no plans to stop over in Chicago, as Red and I had done last summer. J. L. and I had brought a few cans of food with us and I was now experienced in "backdoor bumming," so I knew we wouldn't go hungry. However, our passage through Chicago was not without interruption.

As the freight we were riding pulled into the Chicago yards, a small army of railroad bulls leaped aboard and rounded up about thirty bums, hobos and assorted other illegal passengers. They herded us to a deserted part of the yard, lined us up and began moving down the line beating and clubbing the helpless men standing there. The memory of the wretched bum at the hands of the bull in the Toledo yards flashed through my mind as I stood, trembling, waiting for the bulls to reach me. The sound of the clubs and the pistol barrels on the heads and shoulders of the men and their sharp cries of pain and the moans and groans as they collapsed onto the gravel is still sharp and clear more than a half century later. And well it should be, it was a sound I would hear many times during my years on the road.

To my astonishment, when the cops got to J. L. and me, they grabbed us by the scruff of the neck, twirled us around and placed several well-aimed kicks to our backsides.

"Now, git, and don't come back here," the leader of the bulls shouted at us.

We took off at a full run, neither slowing down nor looking back until we were well clear of the railroad property. Later, I would learn that the bulls continued to beat the men they had captured, finally arresting some of them and releasing those who had been most severely injured in the attack.

This was my second experience at being "ass kicked,"

by railroad cops and I was damned tired of it. But, considering the fate of the others, I couldn't help but feel we had been very lucky to have come away with nothing more than injured pride and sore asses.

Although we both felt like men and could work like men, at fifteen we weren't men and didn't look the part. And even in those brutal times, beating a child was considered a serious matter and could mean nothing but trouble for the cop. While there were many railroad bulls who were not intimidated by this official prohibition, who wouldn't hesitate to shoot a kid right between the eyes if he caught him on a freight, most tended to do little more than give us a good, swift boot and send us on our way. We would have contact with both types this summer.

As we happily left Chicago behind, there were other threats to our safety of which we knew very little but would learn about quickly. Jimmy Lester and I boarded what we thought to be an empty boxcar headed for Omaha only to discover it was occupied by a dirty, unpleasant-looking wino, sprawled on the floor, his head propped up against the wall, his grubby fingers clutching an empty bottle.

"Hello, boys. Where ya headed?"

"Omaha," I replied, moving with J. L. to the opposite end of the car.

"Hey, boys, come on down here where we can talk, plenty of room."

"That's okay," J. L. replied, "we want to get some sleep."

We laid down on a large piece of cardboard and closed our eyes, pretending to sleep. I kept my eyes open just a slit, keeping watch on the wino who, for several minutes, sat staring at us. In the dim light I could see his face, slack-jawed, his tongue partially protruding through a wide gap created by a number of missing lower teeth. After perhaps ten minutes had passed, the wino slowly climbed on unsteady legs and quietly crept in our direction. I lay motionless, closing my eyes tight, as though I was sound asleep. Although I didn't know it, J. L. was doing the same. I could hear the wino's rasping breath as he leaned down to us and I could smell the sour vomit and urine that impregnated his filthy clothes.

He remained poised there for a long moment and then he whispered: "Boy, you wanna have some fun?" Then I felt his hand on my leg, near the crotch. Like a sprung bear trap, my arm came up to snag him in a choke hold.

"Ya want some fun, huh?" I said, squeezing tighter.

The wino struggled and screamed to be turned loose, but I wasn't ready to let him go.

By this time J. L. was on his feet and had hold of the wino's arm, pulling him to a standing position. I kept my grip on him as J. L. and I marched him to the open boxcar door. Without a word between us, J. L. and I knew what we were going to do. At the door, I released the wino just as J. L. unloaded a vicious right to the man's face, knocking him off the speeding train. We looked after him, saw him hit the roadbed next to the tracks and tumble over several times before coming to rest in a heap as we sped away in the darkness.

"D' ya think he's killed?" I asked J. L.

"Nah, you can't hurt a drunk; he'll come to after a bit and probably not remember what happened to him."

We would, during other trips, have occasion to employ this same tactic when molested by others on the road. But the "queers" would prove to be the least of our troubles this summer.

A few days later, as we were slowly pulling into Hoisington, Kansas, in a boxcar crowded with about twenty sleeping men, a bull jumped in, a club in one hand and a pistol in the other, and began shooting into the floor while screaming at the top of his voice: "Get out'a here, get out'a here."

Most of us had been rolled up in blankets, our shoes off and tied around our necks. As the men jumped up and moved to the open doors on each side of the car still in stocking feet, the bull clubbed them viciously in the back or on the head as they jumped off the train. I managed to get my own shoes on, slipping under the bull's arm and jumping before he could swing at me. J. L. had gone out the opposite door, much to his later regret.

The train was moving less than ten miles an hour, just fast enough to cause you to stumble ahead, trying to keep your balance. J. L. had no sooner hit the ground and taken two or three steps when he ran smack into a five-foot-tall track switch. He smashed face-first into the round steel direction indicator at the top of the switch. The impact split his forehead open from the hairline to the bridge of his nose, broke his nose and blackened both eyes, which were soon swollen closed. Knocked unconscious, he lay crumpled alongside the tracks, where he was found by three or four hobos, who picked him up and carried him to their jungle.

Having jumped from the other side of the train, I had to wait for more than five minutes for the very long, slow-moving freight to get by me. By that time, J. L. was nowhere to be seen. I wandered around for a short time, calling him but receiving no response. I was unaware of his accident and assumed that he had quickly left the yards to escape the bulls.

We had agreed when we left Toledo that should we become separated along the route, we would meet at the nearest train depot or post office. I went into the weeds and bedded down for the night, planning to seek out J. L. in the morning.

Until noon the next day I shuttled back and forth between the depot and the post office looking for J. L. without success. Finally, in the early afternoon, I found the local jungle and there, surrounded by sympathetic hobos attempting to minister to his wounds, sat a dazed and confused Jimmy Lester OdNeal.

He looked awful, his forehead laid open and smeared

with clotted and dried blood, his nose pushed over to one side, his eyelids terribly swollen and nearly shut, and the flesh all around them was a ghastly purple.

"By God, J. L., you look pitiful bad," I said, then asked: "Why didn't you meet me at the depot?"

He looked up at me, studying me from out of tiny slits where his eyes should be. It seemed to take several seconds before he was able to recognize me.

"Was I supposed to?" he inquired, finally.

"Do you know who I am?"

"Sure do."

"Do you know where you are?"

"Hell, no! All I know for certain is I woke up this mornin' with one hell of a headache and a face that looks like sausage meat."

It took J. L. two days to clear the cobwebs from his brain; we got his nose straightened out and bound up his forehead, and the swelling around his eyes went down within a few days, but he kept a distinctive bluish tinge under his eyes throughout the summer.

A few days later we were on a freight that stopped at Pine Bluffs, Wyoming, when the local sheriff and several of his deputies nabbed us. It was here that we were introduced to a special custom that was observed in many small towns throughout the West and the South.

The sheriff marched the two of us a few blocks to the town jail where a truck was waiting, loaded with ten or twelve men—all vagrants.

"Here's two more for you," the sheriff advised a deputy, shoving us toward the back of the truck.

"Where we goin'?" I asked.

"Why, you're goin' out in the country to pick potatoes," the sheriff said, almost sweetly.

On the way out of town I learned from a couple of the vagrants that the sheriff and the farmers had an arrangement whereby whenever there was a crop to be harvested the sheriff would supply the necessary field hands. The trains would be watched carefully and anyone caught riding the freights would be arrested and pressed into service. The farmers paid several dollars a day for each hand he supplied and the sheriff gave each prisoner fifty cents a day and a bag of Bull Durham cigarette tobacco. Depending on the agreement reached between them, the farmers or the sheriff would feed the men. After a day's work in the fields, the men would be trucked back to the town jail where they would be locked up for the night. The "sentence" to be served was however long it took to pick or harvest the area's crops—usually fifteen to thirty days.

We were taken to a huge farm seven or eight miles from town where we were ordered into the fields to pick potatoes. There were men already at work and with our group the entire force numbered about forty. A single deputy with a shotgun was left to guard us.

We were told to start down the rows, putting the unearthed potatoes into gunny sacks. The rows were very long—from a half mile to a mile—and the pickers were well spread out.

"I ain't going to be any man's slave," I quietly told J. L. "We're not goin' to spend fifteen days pickin' potatoes for these guys for a lousy fifty cents a day. When we get to the end of the row we'll look the fencerow over and if there's good enough shelter from buckshot, we're gettin' out of here."

We picked to the end of the row and saw that the fencerow sloped down to a small creek with trees lining both banks and a good deal of excellent cover.

"We'll pick around once more and when we get down here again, we'll make a break for it."

I had gone hunting with my father many times and knew the effective range of a shotgun, how far we'd have to be from the guard before making a run for it.

I wasn't afraid of being shot; I was more worried about what would happen to us if we weren't able to make a clean getaway and were caught by the deputy.

Reaching the end of the field, I made a quick check on

the guard and saw that he was far up the row. "NOW, J. L.," I shouted and bolted for the fencerow.

I expected to hear the blast of the shotgun any second, but it never came. As we leaped over the fence and headed down the bank, across the creek and into the trees, we heard the voices of the other pickers raised in a loud chorus of, "Go boys, go!"

We followed the creek for about a mile before coming upon a road where we were able to hitchhike back to town and catch the first westbound freight that came through. We'd escaped an illegal work gang . . . but not for the last time.

The jungles along the way were familiar and comfortable. A few times we ran into 'bos I'd met the previous summer. They were always happy to see me and welcomed us into their camps.

"Often wondered how you made out, boy," one of them told me. This time, when we gathered around the campfire in the evening, I had adventures of my own to tell.

Jimmy Lester took to the hobos and they seemed to like him.

We arrived in Emmett a little over a week after leaving Toledo—no speed record, but still, not too bad considering the interruptions we'd met on the way.

My sister Alice was now married to a German immigrant named Jake Ritter, a very fine man whom I liked immediately. They were still taking care of mother, whose health was continuing to deteriorate. J. L. and I stayed with them for a short time, but it became obvious that we were imposing on their hospitality. So, as soon as we found work, we left, spending the summer sleeping in barns, hay stacks or on the ground.

Jimmy Lester was a good farm hand, having spent his life working in the fields as I had, and at fifteen we both could do a man's work, could harness horses and work them all day, knew how to use farm machinery, equipment and wagons, could pick potatoes or fruit or okra or beans. So, we had no trouble getting work right away.

The farms and ranches in the area grew a great deal of hay which was well irrigated, thus producing several "cuttings" a year. We spent most of the summer working through the hay district. It was savage and merciless work, definitely not for the soft or unseasoned. But J. L. and I thrived on it, giving our labor in full measure.

Our recreational moments received the same dedicated attention. We spent each Saturday night in towns such as Emmett and Caldwell and, occasionally, Boise, and we made the most of our visits there. A traveling carnival came to the area one weekend during the summer and J. L. and I reveled in the festivities it offered. In a tent a man of perhaps twenty-one came out on the stage and offered to wrestle or box any man interested in testing his strength or abilities.

"I'll give ten dollars to any man who will try me," he announced to the capacity crowd. "And to the man who can beat me will go one half of the gate receipts for this performance."

"Challenge him, Maury," Jimmy Lester urged. "Go ahead, you can whip him at rasslin'."

The man was heavier than I—I weighed about 135 pounds at that time—and he was obviously in excellent physical condition. But, working in the fields had made me hard and strong, and my wrestling experience, I knew, somewhat balanced out his greater size. I was about to accept his offer when a burly, fierce-looking man in the audience stepped up and offered to box him.

The challenger removed his shirt and was assisted into a pair of light-weight boxing gloves. It took the "carnie" man less than two minutes to lay the challenger out cold; a vicious right to the forehead, a sharp left and a thundering right to the jaw and the big farmer was flat on his back unconscious.

I had a moment's hesitation but then thought, what the hell, all he can do is pin me.

I could see right away that he was more a brawler than a fancy wrestler. I gave him a couple of "slip-arounds," ducking under his arms and getting behind him and finally managed to leap onto his back with my arms securely fastened around his neck, pulling his head hard to the left, and my legs locked around his legs in what was called a "figure four." Firmly attached to the man, I determined to just hang on until he wore himself out.

He pitched and jumped and flung himself around the stage trying everything he could to dislodge me, but I hung on like I was riding a wild bull. He screamed and moaned and groaned but I wouldn't let loose. He grunted and fumed and cussed but my hold was so securely locked that I couldn't have let go even if I had wanted to, and after five or ten minutes of total frustration the man had become so enraged I was certain that if I released him, he'd probably kill me.

Finally, thoroughly spent, the carnie man signaled "uncle." I had defeated him. Years later, the image of me clinging for dear life to the man's back could still bring tears of laughter to old Jake Ritter's eyes.

I waited until the tent had cleared out before asking for my share of the gate.

"Well, now, I don't think the match was a proper one," the carnival manager told me. "You didn't actually wrestle my man, you just clamped on his back and hung on. This weren't no rodeo. I don't think we have to pay you anything."

"Well, you're gonna pay me," I insisted. "I've got about a hundred friends out there, and I know a lot more people around here. So, you're gonna pay, one way or the other."

The manager thought for a moment while several of his "roustabouts" began gathering around us. He was trying to decide whether I was serious and whether a possible all-out riot was worth saving a few bucks. With a deep sigh of resignation, he said: "Okay, young fella." He reached into his coat pocket and brought out a ten-dollar bill.

"What's this? I'm supposed to get half of the gate receipts."

"And that's what you got, that's half of the gate."

I knew they had probably taken in several hundred dollars, but it was now my time to consider whether further confrontation was worth it; I hadn't been totally candid with the carnie manager. I didn't have a "hundred friends" waiting outside; I had just J. L. and my brother-in-law, Jake, and he was something of a pacifist who didn't like trouble of any kind.

"Oh, well, so I got skinned by a carnie," I muttered, pocketing the ten dollars. "Just like thousands of others."

I had beaten the guy fair and square and the thought of calling in the police had crossed my mind, but I abandoned the idea; the cops had probably been paid off by the carnival operators to avoid being run out of town—the police wouldn't be interested in helping me. Besides, I had already had my fill of contact with small town police, both in Wyoming and here in Idaho.

A few weeks prior to the carnival incident, J. L. and I had gone into Caldwell for some Saturday night fun. Prohibition had just been repealed and saloon operators, in an apparent attempt to make up for a lot of lost time, weren't too critical of who they served. Although we looked a little older than our fifteen years, we certainly didn't appear to be old enough to be served beer. But we found that, in a busy bar on Saturday night, no one questioned us too carefully.

We thought it was pretty "smooth" to have a few beers and this cockiness got a little out of control. J. L. and I never went looking for fights; we didn't believe in starting trouble. But, whether it was something we said or whether our manner just irritated some young men in a Caldwell tavern, we suddenly found ourselves in a full-blown barroom brawl. The next thing we knew, one of the local sheriff's deputies was dragging Jimmy Lester and me out of the place, telling us we were under arrest.

"We didn't start it," I protested. "Why ain't you arresting the other guys, too?"

It was a foolish question; the local boys were never arrested for fighting with a couple of drifters.

We were thrown in the town jail and locked up. We assumed it was only until the next morning, when we would be turned loose and ordered out of town. But Sunday morning no one came to let us out; no one showed up to bring us breakfast or even water to drink. By Sunday afternoon, when we were still alone and unfed, we began yelling at the top of our lungs for someone to come and feed us, to bring us a drink of water. But no one appeared. Sunday evening and all of Sunday night we were left alone without so much as a check on us to be certain that we were still locked up.

Finally, Monday morning, we heard noises in the sheriff's office.

"Hey! Come in here!" I shouted, as though I were calling my butler.

The Sheriff opened the door to his office and peered into the tiny cell block. He looked puzzled.

"What the hell are you guys doin' in here?"

"Well, we sure didn't break in; we been in here without food or water for two days. What's the idea of leavin' us like that?"

He replied: "I didn't even know you was in here."

"Your damned deputy put us in here Saturday night."

"Well, he got off and went home and never told me about you fellas, and nobody comes in on Sunday."

"Doggone!" I said. "We're about to die in here."

The sheriff hurriedly unlocked the cell door, let us out and then rushed off to get us breakfast. Later he apologized profusely and turned us loose.

"Well," J. L. said, as we dashed back to the farm where we were working that week. "We thought we were gonna be real smart and drink some beer and have some fun. But all we got was beat up by the locals and thrown in jail by the law."

Such was small town justice in the 1930s.

As the harvest season wound down, J. L. and I decided

we'd start back for Toledo a bit early so we could take the southern route back and see more of the country, as I had done the year before. Jimmy had relatives in Lawrenceburg, Tennessee, that he wanted to visit.

I went around to Jake and Alice's to say goodbye and to see my mother once more. I had no idea, as I took my leave, promising to see mother next summer, that I would never see her again. Before the snow was off the ground the next spring, she had died, released at last from the torment of a wasted body.

• • •

The men who rode the freights during the Depression often roamed mindlessly across the country, with no destination to reach and no schedule to keep. It was not at all unusual to see a train headed in one direction, loaded with transients traveling in search of work, pass another train, with just as many job seekers aboard, going in the opposite direction, neither group knowing that there was no work either way.

Jimmy Lester and I had gotten off a southbound freight in a small Colorado town and had walked over to the depot to sit on the benches for a while and chat with a number of hobos who were sunning themselves. An old hobo had gotten off the same train we had come in on. He sat next to us and engaged the other 'bos in idle chatter. Then, looking up, he spotted a train passing slowly through the depot.

"Will you look at all that nice paper in there?" he said, indicating the open door of one of the boxcars. The walls were lined with a brown paper that was installed to prevent grain from spilling out. It was known as "thousand-mile paper" because it was of heavy construction, could be torn off the walls, rolled up and taken away to use to lie on or cover up with. It held up very well and could last for a thousand miles of travel.

Boxcars with thousand-mile paper were much sought after because the paper insured a cleaner, more comfortable, ride than most other cars, which tended to be dirty and not as nice to ride in.

The old hobo was so thrilled to see the attractively clean car that he jumped up, saying: "I believe I'll catch that train." He ran off, quickly overtaking the slow-moving freight, and managed to haul himself aboard the car with the thousand-mile paper. With a broad grin on his face, he waved happily to the rest of us.

"That damned fool," one of the other hobos said, laughing. "That train's headed back the way he just come from."

But it didn't matter to the old man; he didn't care which direction the train was taking, he was "goin' just to be goin'." That was the attitude of a great many men on the road back then. It was unimportant where you went; when you saw a nice, clean car lined with thousand-mile paper, it was just too tempting and you felt that you shouldn't let it get away from you.

Jimmy Lester and I were nabbed twice more on the trip back by sheriffs recruiting work gangs for farm harvests, and both times we escaped the first day by simply taking off and outrunning the buckshot. In both cases, the guards actually shot at us, although I was never certain whether they had aimed at us or fired over our heads.

The second time we were caught was near Houston, Texas. We'd gotten off a train on the outskirts of town to avoid going into the yards where we'd heard there were several very mean bulls. We were resting under a bridge, along with perhaps twelve or fifteen other vagabonds, when a hobo came up to us and said:

"Listen fellas, you want to get away from here right away; they's a bunch of railroad cops prowlin' around here to get men to work on the farms. I know, I just got out from fifteen days on one of their work gangs. I came by here to warn you 'bos about the cops."

He had no sooner finished what he had come to say than a posse of railroad cops and sheriff's deputies swooped down on us and took us into custody—including the hapless hobo who had gone out of his way to try and warn us. He was back for another fifteen days on the very day he had been released.

When we got to the farm where we were supposed to work, I told the guard that I had no intention of working in the fields for a half a buck a day and a bag of tobacco.

"I don't mind working, but I expect to be paid a fair wage for it," I said, resolutely. "If I'm not gonna be paid, then I'm not goin' to stay. . . . No pay—no stay!"

The guard smiled and patted his shotgun, replying, "If you try to leave you'll get some of this."

I just smiled back and moved into the field with J. L., already looking for a possible escape route. Within an hour we were over the fencerow and into a thick patch of woods, headed for the main highway.

"You know," J. L. said, "if that guard had taken you seriously when you said you weren't gonna stay, he might have stayed close enough to put a load of double-aught in both of our asses. Maybe you hadn't better say anything to them the next time."

"I believe in being honest with a man," I replied. But, at the same time, I had to agree with J. L. that taunting the guard could make things hot for us if we were caught by him some time in the future.

We went on to Memphis and then to Lawrenceburg, spending a few days with J. L.'s kin before heading for home.

The last leg of our summer's journey was to be marked by still another confrontation with a railroad bull.

We'd caught a northbound freight out of Cincinnati headed for Toledo. Unable to find an open door, we were sprawled on top of a boxcar. A railroad cop, riding in the engine, saw us jump aboard and came crawling along the catwalks toward us. As he drew near, he pulled out a pistol. This was enough to get us to beat a hasty retreat down into an open, fully loaded coal car. The cop began firing at us as we scampered off the boxcar. By crowding down against the forward pile of coal and just under the overhanging lip of the car we were protected against the bull's pistol fire, but we knew that if he came down into the car, he would have a clean shot at us. To keep him back, we began throwing chunks of coal at him, lobbing them like grenades.

The cop had flattened himself on the catwalk of the boxcar, raising his head every few seconds and firing a shot down at the coal pile we were hiding next to. We continued this mini-war for over twenty minutes, watching the top of the boxcar for the bull's head to rise up and then hurling large chunks of coal until the head was pulled back.

"We can't keep this up all the way to Toledo," I told J. L. "We'd better try to get off this train."

Within a few minutes I felt the train begin to slow and knew we were coming into Dayton; this would be our best chance to escape the bull and his pistol. When the train had slowed to about ten miles an hour, J. L. and I let loose with a huge barrage of coal chunks, keeping the man pinned down on the top of the boxcar. Then, quickly, we scampered up the coal pile and over the edge, moving quickly down the ladder on off the train. The bull, expecting more missiles and keeping down, shielding his head with his arms against the falling chunks, was unaware that we had left the train and were dashing into the woods near the trackside.

While we should have been terribly conscious of how close we had come to being shot and possibly killed, Jimmy Lester and I viewed the experience as just one more adventure we'd be able to tell the kids back at school. We seemed to have been detached from the peril we'd faced, as if we had seen it all in a Saturday afternoon movie matinee at the Ohio Theater in Toledo.

"How was your summer?" my father asked when I arrived home the day before school opened.

I paused, thinking of the bulls in Chicago brutalizing the vagabonds we'd been riding with; I thought about the work gangs into which we'd been unsuccessfully conscripted, and of the sound of the shotgun blasts fired to attempt to prevent our escape; I thought of Jimmy Lester's pitifully mangled face after we'd had to leap from a train to avoid another brutal bull; I thought of the carnie man and my wild ride on his back and of the Caldwell jail where J. L. and I had spent a very lonely weekend; I thought of the battle of the coal pile on the trip from Cincinnati; I thought about the whole adventure-filled summer that had been the most satisfying, most exciting and most rewarding three months of my young life. And then I answered my father's question.

"It was just an ordinary summer, Dad."

CHAPTER 5

IF THE WORLD CALLS YOU A BUM

Probably one of the most troubling public relations problems faced by the hobo—both in the past and in more recent times—is the stubborn misconception that the general public has had regarding hobos, tramps and bums. While the bum doesn't seem to mind being mistaken for a hobo, the feeling is definitely *not* mutual. Nor did tramps of more than forty years ago appreciate being mistaken for the shiftless, lazy and generally worthless individuals "on the bum." Speaking for the hobo, I think it's important that the public understand clearly the difference between a hobo and a bum.

A very intelligent hobo once illustrated the difference with the following story. A bum would come to the back door of a farmhouse and say, "Lady, can you spare a bite to eat?" A hobo, on the other hand, would say, "Lady, could I chop that wood over there in exchange for something to eat?" The hobo was always willing to work, the bum, never.

I was taught by the old hobos in Toledo, and by every other 'bo I met in later years, that a true hobo never forced himself on anyone, that he always considered others. For example, a hobo would approach a boxcar and seeing someone inside, would always ask, "Is this car full?" If the reply was, "Yes, it's full," even if there was just the one man inside, the hobo would move on looking for another freight car rather than force himself on a person who didn't want his company.

This, I've found, typified the true hobo, and the hobos I knew exemplified this natural courtesy and consideration for others that earned them the title, "Knights of the Road."

Some hobos eventually left the road to become famous in other pursuits. Jack London, Ernest Hemingway, U.S. Supreme Court Justice William O. Douglas, Winthrop Rockefeller and Clark Gable are just a few of those who once rode the freights.

On pleasant nights around a jungle camp fire I listened as the older 'bos talked of the men they had known when they walked in younger men's shoes or of men they had heard other brothers speak about so fondly.

Reading Red spent, as far as anyone could determine, more than forty years from the late 1800s until 1933, riding the boxcars of the Pennsy railroad. He eked out a modest existence doing yard chores in small towns between Allentown, Pennsylvania, and Youngstown, Ohio. Each summer he could be seen, a burly man with a thick shock of wavy red hair, his bedroll on one shoulder, shuffling from railroad yard to the town's "main stem" where he would call on the barber, the blacksmith or gas station owner, the hardware store proprietor and the chief fireman, spending a few pleasant minutes with each, chatting about the weather or politics. His exact age was unknown but was estimated at between 65 and 70.

The people of the towns he called on found him extremely friendly, always pleasant and scrupulously honest. He sometimes smoked a pipe but did not drink and was never heard to utter profanity. He always had a cheery wave for the men and the children and never failed to bow genteelly and doff his old, battered hat when meeting a woman. The men found him extremely knowledgeable and articulate but never argumentative.

Red was greeted warmly wherever he went and was considered a genius in the flower garden. Calling just two or three times during the late summer and spring and once in the fall to prepare the beds for the coming winter, Red was able to produce the most beautiful violets, daisies, cowslips, geraniums and begonias seen in the East. It was said that he had a special touch which drew thriving, robust life from the most imperfect soil; he spoke softly and lovingly to the buds and the blossoms, encouraging them to flourish. He never took money for his labors, accepting only a meal or perhaps an occasional pouch of pipe tobacco or an old magazine or a book. He slept in barns or work sheds when the weather was bad but usually in a small grove of trees and wild flowers that could always be found on the edge of the towns he visited. He did his bathing and personal laundry in a local stream or brook and spent evenings in the town park or the library if there was one.

No one knew where Red came from originally or where he disappeared to each winter; he resisted every attempt to question him about his personal life. And he refused every offer of a place to stay and a job to carry him through the winter, saying that he had places to go and things to do elsewhere.

When the spring of 1933 came and went with no sign of Reading Red people along the rail lines in central Pennsylvania grew more concerned with each passing day. He didn't make any of his usual stops that summer nor during the following year. He was a major topic of conversation in the towns and villages those two years; rumors circulated freely, suggesting that he had been killed in a train wreck near Sharon, Pennsylvania, or that he had been arrested for illegally riding the freights and had been sentenced to a chain gang, or that he had met a rich widow and had settled down.

It was not until 1937 that the word began to filter into the mountains and valleys of the Allegheny Mountains explaining why Reading Red no longer called on them. A newly arrived resident to the area heard of the citizen's concern over the disappearance of the old hobo, demonstrated an interest in the mystery and was shown several photos in which Red appeared. The new resident looked at the photos and announced that she knew what had happened to him and also who he really was.

Reading Red was actually a wealthy financier who sought to escape the pressures of business by dressing in worn clothes and climbing aboard a freight train—belonging to a railroad in which he owned a large block of stock—and spending a few months each year in total anonymity, enjoying contact with "ordinary people," and tending their lawns and flower gardens. He had stopped making his annual rounds, the people who profited from his abilities learned, when a debilitating stroke robbed him of strength and mobility. And in 1935, he had died. The beautiful flowers he had so carefully nurtured never bloomed as well as when Reading Red had spoken to them softly and lovingly.

There were, over the years, many stories circulating about other colorful hobos who made a lasting impression on the people they met, sometimes in the most unexpected places.

• • •

In 1970, a group of Harvard University students invited a hobo in off the streets of Cambridge, Massachusetts, to have Thanksgiving dinner as their guest. The hobo stayed for the next fifteen years, hidden by the students from university officials and police.

The hobo was Damon Paine, a part-time handyman and a chain-smoking meat-eater who was taken in by the residents of the vegetarian Dudley Cooperative House on the Harvard campus.

Paine—who if he had a road name never gave it to his university patrons—smoked six packs of cigarettes a day and spurned the vegetables offered him in favor of steak. He told the students that he had spent the Depression years riding the rails across America, worked in shipyards during World War II and was a cook for a time. He was a first-class bridge player and an expert auto mechanic, assisting his benefactors in repairing their cars. He also contributed his Social Security checks to buy food for the house.

Despite his outspoken and usually negative opinion of Harvard University and the "snobs" who studied there, he remained there until 1984 when it was discovered that he had bone morrow cancer. The students continued to care for him, seeing that he had medical treatment and blood transfusions. The students voted to take care of Paine until the end and appointed one student to take charge of his care.

"It's hard to explain," one student said later. "He was a gruff man who would say what he thought. But he was a human being and a friend."

He died on April 2, 1985, with no relatives, no property, and no will. A Harvard University professor donated a cemetery plot and a local undertaker supplied his services. Sixty members of the cooperative attended Paine's funeral and planted a maple tree in his memory. In his room, students found pages of poetry in Paine's handwriting. The students had no idea he had such an interest or an ability.

"There's a certain kind of mystery in this," one of the students said. "He made a difference . . . it will have an indelible effect on all of (us) . . ."

In the twenty years that I traveled the "iron road" I got to know several hundred professional hobos. About two dozen of that number stood out as very special—men like Fry Pan Jack, Slow-Motion Shorty, Mountain Dew and Hood River Blackie—individuals who had that peculiar quality to their character that made them unforgettable.

John Fisk was known as Fry Pan Jack (some called him Fryin' Pan Jack). He was the best fireside cook I ever knew; he made the best hobo stew this side of hobo heaven.

Hard and tough as granite, he'd been in the navy as a young man, going on the road after his service time had been completed. He'd rambled up and down the West Coast as a part-time stevedore, spending his winters in Seattle, Washington, traveling the road for over fifty years and riding freights until 1986.

In 1985, Fry Pan was appointed King of the Hobos when the elected king for that year suddenly died. We were all glad he had been so honored. He certainly deserved the title and, apparently, it came just in time.

In August, 1986, as he was preparing to leave for the annual National Hobo's Convention in Britt, Iowa, Fry Pan suffered a severe heart attack. He underwent bypass surgery and has had a slow but steady recovery since. But Britt in August isn't the same without him.

• • •

One of my dearest hobo friends was Arthur William Parker, whose road name was Slow-Motion Shorty because that's how he moved. Shorty first went on the road at the age of 16 when his grandmother—his only surviving relative—died, leaving him with nowhere to go. Following a brief hitch in the navy, he'd spent the rest of his life hoboing.

Shorty never had a trade or profession. Once, when asked what he had done to help the war effort during World War II, he replied that he'd set pins in a bowling alley.

He was a gentle, simple man who often impressed people as not too bright. Yet he had almost total recall, particularly in the area of baseball. He could recite names of players and their records back to the turn of the century and was able to tick off club statistics like he had a computer in his head. I've often heard him correct someone who had erred in statements about a particular ball club, or ball game or a specific player, and he was always proven right.

He also demonstrated a remarkable memory for the names and faces of children who came to the hobo convention in Britt over a period of several years. While many of us were able to remember some of the faces of people we had met the previous year, Shorty could walk up and call forty or fifty kids by name. Naturally they were extremely flattered and absolutely adored him. His keen knowledge of railroad geography was another of his remarkable talents.

Shorty was elected hobo king twice—in 1969 and again in 1974. He delighted in his terms of office; in 1974 he carried with him business cards he'd had printed which proclaimed his exalted title.

He was born in Rochelle, Illinois, and returned to the town each year to "winter up" in a cheap hotel near the bus depot where he worked now and then as a "baggage boy."

In his $58-a-month room he kept an electric coffee percolator which he used to heat water for instant coffee. But he often felt confined during the long, bitter winter of the plains and would hike down to the trackside and make some coffee the "right way," over an open fire in a tin can.

He'd owned a collapsible Sterno stove. But—in a fit of typical soft-hearted generosity—he'd given it to an old hobo traveling companion, Connecticut Slim, when he came through town.

In 1981 Shorty was awarded supplemental Social Security and moved into a senior citizens center in Sacramento, California. The hard years on the road were taking their toll on his slight and frail body. And while he longed to join us in Britt each August, his declining health simply would not permit it.

• • •

John Mislen was born "somewhere in the East" in 1905. In his youth he had mined lead in Colorado, an occupation that inspired his hobo road name, "Hard Rock Kid." He was a solitary type who, in his later years, wore a long, scraggly beard and was accused of being a "close-mouthed old devil" by some who knew him. Still, everybody truly liked him.

The Kid had left Trenton, New Jersey, when he was seventeen because of an unhappy home life. In addition to working in a lead mine, the Kid had been a construction boomer and a cowboy.

After roaming aimlessly around the country for thirty years or more he finally settled on the state of Iowa as his permanent territory. He traveled in a circle through the state, stopping in small hamlets, staying a day or two here and moving on to spend a day or two in the next town. He became well known and liked in many small towns, villages and cities in Iowa, and although there were numerous places where he'd be welcome to spend the night, he so loved the outdoor life, he always chose to sleep out under the stars.

The Kid was elected King of the Hobos five times; in 1965, 1967, 1970, 1972 and 1975. In August, wherever he might be, he'd cut short his stay to attend the convention in Britt.

No one knew much about his past, but that's not unusual with hobos, who are naturally secretive about their personal lives. But some who knew him better than others were curious about his habit of traveling to Ames the first of every month. There were those who believed that the Kid had a Social Security or pension check coming in there.

One of the Kid's favorite spots in Iowa was Ogden, a town of about 2,000. People there knew him well and welcomed his visits.

Bernice Muench, an older woman who worked in the Coffee Pot, a Main Street diner, said: "The business people befriended him and always looked forward to the time of year when the Kid would be coming through. You couldn't help but like him; he enjoyed his life so much."

• • •

Most hobos traveled pretty light, taking only those items that they needed to survive on the road: a blanket, a couple changes of clothes, some heavy paper—"thousand-mile paper," if they could get it—a pencil and some paper, a toothbrush, several pairs of socks and perhaps a few cooking utensils.

Some carried next to nothing, choosing a briefcase or small satchel, or maybe nothing at all. Such men were known as "streamliners," traveling in a hurry, getting there quickly. It was difficult to tell they were hobos.

Others carried heavy baggage, including the tools of their trade, work clothes and work boots. This weighty luggage was known as a "Montana bindle," and often contained just about everything the hobo owned.

• • •

Many hobos were intelligent, talented men. Feather River John rode the rails for years when he was a young man. Later, under his real name, John McClaughry, he ran for and was elected to the Vermont state legislature. He has worked long and hard in the interest of hobos; he was the creator of the Hobo Foundation, a non-profit organization whose goal is to establish a home for aged vagabonds. He hopes for a retirement spot somewhere in the Southwest, "in a warm climate with maybe a few old railroad cars parked on a siding or some simple board shacks with cookstoves. A place where old-timers could sit around and tell stories of the good old days when they rode the high iron."

John believes, as I do, that old hobos want to avoid being put in an institution, "hovered over by candy-stripers and welfare workers. They would just as soon die out underneath a viaduct, along the tracks in the free air where they've lived all their lives."

In 1975 the foundation was officially formed and had its first and only board meeting in an abandoned slaughterhouse in Britt. I was named president, Hood River Blackie vice-president and Feather River John, secretary-treasurer. John admits that the bylaws are written so that the secretary-treasurer actually runs the foundation.

Because of the many legal problems connected with this enterprise, not a great deal has been accomplished. But all the old hobos think a retirement home for 'bos is a great idea and have hopes that someday it will become a reality.

• • •

Lonesome Whistle, who still lives in Fort Worth, Texas, left the road to become an attorney. To relax, he still dons old clothes, goes down to the freight yards and hops a freight for a short trip. It's very hard to get the itch to travel out of the hobo.

• • •

James "Big Town" Gorman picked up spare change sharpening knives and scissors. But not just anyone's scissors; he serviced the shears of some of the most important men in the world. "I sharpened Truman's scissors, I sharpened Eisenhower's scissors and Kennedy's scissors. Whenever I was in Washington, I'd sharpen the president's scissors. Except Nixon—I never got to sharpen his."

Big Town never learned to drive a car, never received Social Security or a pension, didn't drink or smoke and read two newspapers every day. He had a remarkable knowledge and understanding of the stock market. Scissor Sam was another hobo who made his way sharpening scissors for people along his circuit.

• • •

Probably the most brilliant hobo I ever knew was Ralph Gooding, whose road name, Hood River Blackie, came from his head of coal-black hair and the town of Hood River, Oregon, where he used to pick apples and pears.

His interest in hoboing began on the West Coast when he was ten and began hanging around freight yards. He commenced a career as a hobo at age fourteen after his stepfather angrily hurled a pitchfork at him. An old hobo took him under his wing and taught him the hobo rules and much of the hobo history.

Blackie had only an eighth-grade education but was later tested at a university and found to possess an IQ of 146, a near genius. He became the hobo's historian, collecting over the years 610 biographies of men of the iron road. He had plans to publish a four-volume set of stories about "unknown Americans." The first volume was to be titled *The Passing of the Hobo.*

When asked why he had undertaken such a monumental task, Blackie replied: "I believe I'm capable of preserving the memory of the hobo; I'm the youngest and I have the best chance of completing it."

Unfortunately, his chance wasn't so good after all. In 1984 Blackie died before his ambition could be realized. His research, the more than 600 hobo biographies and his unfinished manuscript, gathers dust somewhere. He was only 59 years old.

• • •

Tim "Connecticut Slim" Moylan was a tall, lanky man who always wore the sad, pained expression of one who had suffered greatly. More than forty years on the road cost him his home, his marriage and the love of his children. He had seen only one of his grandchildren and wasn't certain exactly how many he had. He claimed he had been afflicted with what he called "drapetomania," a disease which he said caused a morbid desire to wander and made him prefer the searching in life to the finding.

He'd begun hoboing before the great stock market crash of 1929; he'd been on the road when the St. Valentine's Day massacre took place; he once was in a Montana hobo jungle when Jack Dempsey took on a group of local toughs. He'd lived on every major skid row in the country, had been a singing waiter, bartender, club steward, carnival barker and salesman of a number of suspicious items and products, including a powder that he claimed would kill every moth and flea in your home.

He once worked with a professional pickpocket. They would enter a bar, the pickpocket would suddenly go into a wild "Yiddish" song and dance, twirling around the room and expertly relieving the customers of their valuables, which he would then pass on to Slim.

"Folks were so overwhelmed they didn't notice he was picking their pockets," Slim recalled. "I was his standby man. When he made a hit he'd run by and slip me the stuff. We really made a team."

In his travels he had worked in the Salinas Valley of California with the migrant workers depicted in John Steinbeck's novels and in the wheat fields of the Great Plains, and he'd danced with go-go girls at the hobo convention in Britt.

Slim had a long and colorful career as a hobo, but his health had been sapped by the years of travel and his longing to be running the line finally faded. Several years ago, Slim decided to retire.

"There's no companionship on the road anymore, no friendship," he said. "You used to stop in a jungle and maybe you'd meet 20 guys and talk over how things are and where you've been. There was a grapevine of information and if you had a good memory you could find out where to go anywhere in the United States."

He believed that hoboing was just about finished. Most of his close friends had caught "the westbound." He had settled in a Parkersburg, West Virginia, boarding house, living on welfare benefits.

"I know lots of guys that go to Los Angeles and stay in them missions. They stay there all winter, eating that old mission soup and drinking wine. They come out skinnier than a rail and half dead and brainwashed from John 3:16."

He said that he would make occasional trips to Ohio and Illinois to see old friends, but there would be no more casual roaming. After nearly a half century on the iron road, Slim had no more interest in the searching; he was content with the finding.

• • •

There were many hobos like Hood River Blackie, who possessed considerable literary talent. One of the most successful of these authors and writers is Irving L. Stevens, also known as Fishbones, a name given him in his youth because of his extremely underfed appearance.

'Bones wrote an entertaining book titled *Hoboing in the 1930s*, which he published himself in 1982.

He was born on June 21, 1910, in East Surry, Maine, and became enthralled with railroads and steam locomotives by the age of nine. He began a hobo career during the Depression of the thirties and spent nine years on the road.

His book provides a useful perspective of life on the iron road during those often-bitter years. Today he lives quietly in Corinna, Maine, where he manufactures an insect repellent and takes an occasional trip, though not in a boxcar.

Fishbones is part of a long and respected list of authors who have spent some time on the road. Ernest Hemingway and Jack London are perhaps the best-known of this group.

In addition to authors, the hobo fraternity has a large

number of poets and songwriters. Woody Guthrie is probably the most famous. Among my personal favorite hobo poets are Charles "Reefer Charlie" Fox, who is also an accomplished author, and Ivan "Ole the 'Bo" Mills.

This is one of Ole's best:

A HOBO'S BALLAD

You ask why I'm a hobo; and why I sleep in a ditch?
It's not because I'm crazy, no, I just don't want to be rich.
Why, I could earn a million bucks and eat 'til I get fat,
But then I'd lose my girlish form and, Oh, I wouldn't
like that.

Now, I could eat off dishes, it's just a matter of choice,
But when I eat from an old tin can there ain't no dishes
to wash.
And I could ride on a Pullman, but there it is again;
The plush they put on those Pullman seats tickles my
sensitive skin.

I might have been a tenor, and maybe hit high "C,"
But I heard one on the radio and that was enough for
me.
Whenever I think of Lincoln, I know I can never forgive
A man who would murder a man like him and let those
tenors live.

Don't need no money to live on, no money for room and
board.
But when I'm gone I'll mean as much as Mr. Henry Ford.
Why I couldn't run the White House, or a mint, I don't
care which,
It's not because I'm crazy; no, I just don't want to be rich.

And here are two favorites by Reefer Charlie:

THE LAST HOBO

I sit by a little campfire, alone
Beside the railroad track.
My pals have all caught the westbound freight
And they won't be coming back.

We never thought when we were young
That the day must surely come
When we'd ride our final westbound freight
To the land beyond the sun.

So thought this ancient vagabond,
I'm the last of a kind to be.
I've worried about this, these many years.
Oh, why did the Lord pick me?

MEMORIES OF THE PAST

Come sit a spell and let us talk
Of the days of long ago,
Of jungle camps and red-ball freights
And 'bos we used to know;

Of working in the harvest fields,
Driving spikes on an extra gang.
Of picking apples in Yakima,
We didn't give a hang;

Of bad bulls that haunted various yards,
Recall the ones we met?
Like the Southern's notorious Memphis Slim,
Or Cheyenne's killer, old Jeff Carr,
The 'bos all knew of him;

And Pistol Pete on the Wabash
At Little Moberly, Mo;
Julesburg Red the crazy dick,
And Rock Island's Blinky Joe.

They're all gone now, where bad bulls go.
But let us wish them well,
Let's show more mercy than they ever did,
For I'm sure they're all in Hell.

• • •

In addition to the writers and poets and composers among the hobos there is at least one cartoon hobo who rides freight trains all over the North American continent and as far away as China.

Herbert A. Mayer, Jr. was a switchman-conductor with the Terminal Railroad of St. Louis. For twenty-five years Mayer chalked the figure of a sombrero-wearing figure, wrapped in a *serape*, squatting with his back against a palm tree, head bowed in a *siesta*. Under the drawing was always chalked the single name: "Herby" and the date the cartoon was drawn there.

"Herby" was drawn on more than 75,000 railroad freight cars that traveled every standard gauge Western Hemisphere railroad from Mexico City to Fairbanks, Alaska, from the Atlantic to the Pacific Oceans over a quarter of a century. Hobos and railroad employees alike came to know and look for "Herby" rumbling along the mainlines of America.

Mayer kept his identity as creator and artist of "Herby" a secret throughout his years as a railroad employee because he enjoyed hearing the comments of people who had seen his creation without realizing that he was the man responsible. But his secret came out in 1981 when he and his wife traveled to China and he chalked "Herby" on cars of the government-owned railroad of the Peoples' Republic of China.

In 1982, when he attended the hobo convention in Britt, he was hailed as a full celebrity and proclaimed "Grand Duke of the Hobos" for his special contribution to railroading.

Although Mayer has long since retired, "Herby" continues to ride the rails on a few of the cars that stubbornly hold on to the fading little figure. "Herby" also adorned the side of at least one Lincoln Continental, painted by Mayer at the owner's request during the 1982 Britt convention.

• • •

It would take many volumes to fully cover all the hobos I've known; each is different, each has his or her own peculiar qualities, each, his or her own fascinating story to tell.

I think, for example, of Adolf Vandertie, the Hobo Whittler who, with nothing more than a pocket knife, can produce an ornate wooden cage complete with a perfectly formed ball inside, all made from a single block of wood and without disconnecting or gluing—simply by carving the ball inside the cage. He has made this beautiful creation in neckerchief slides and in small pendants and even smaller earring sets. His incredible talent was featured in a "Ripley's Believe It or Not" newspaper column.

"Frisco Jack" Sopko, a hobo king in 1985 and 1986, also comes quickly to mind. He was the only man I ever knew who could splice a stainless steel cable in a ring with absolutely no indications where the wire was connected. Jack had been a sailor when canvas was still used to power ships. When canvas went out of use he hoboed around the country for a time and then became a telephone company cable splicer. After retiring, he again went on the road.

Then there was Charles Arthur Troxel—called Mountain Dew because he made coffee cups from Mountain Dew pop cans. And Larry "Gas Can Paddy" Meirhoff, who one day found himself standing with a large group of men trying to hitch a ride with absolutely no success. He disappeared into a nearby gas station and emerged with a red gasoline can. Holding the empty can where it was easily visible and sticking out his thumb, he received an offer of a ride from the very next motorist to pass by. The can became a piece of permanent equipment and gave him his road name. He used the can for decades; who can pass up someone who's run out of gas?

These were members of a truly special breed of men, the likes of which we are not likely to see again. As the hobo of the past disappears he is replaced by a different kind of individual. And while there are a few young men traveling the country who seem to have the dedication to the spirit that inspired the hobos of fifty years past, they are a distinct minority among the wanders of today's America. Most others are bums . . . cutthroats, thieves and dopeheads who will—and have—slit throats for small change.

It is unlikely that there will ever again be a Virginia Slim, or a Sparky Smith, or an A-No. 1, the Rambler. Even colorful names such as Natchez Trace and Lord Open Road seem beyond the imagination of today's youth —unless, that is, they're naming rock groups.

CHAPTER 6

DO NOT THINK ABOUT TOMORROW

During the summer of 1933 Jimmy Lester OdNeal and I traveled back to Idaho, working the harvests for three months and then making our way back to Toledo just in time to go back to school. J. L.'s family had moved back to Lawrenceburg, Tennessee, and he planned to join them there. We decided to hobo around the South for a while and then he would head for Lawrenceburg and I would continue on for the rest of the summer. I would miss him later, and often I would hop a freight and go to visit him; I did that for several years.

By 1933, when I was sixteen years old, I was, for all intents and purposes, a man. Although I was only five feet seven inches tall and weighed just 145 pounds, I was as solid and as strong as any man. My winters in the Toledo YMCA wrestling program kept me in top physical condition. I was continuing to win city amateur wrestling championships and felt confident about being able to handle myself in any situation on the road.

During the last two trips J. L. and I took together we needed to be in good shape; we were no longer kids and weren't mistaken for such. There were many occasions when we had to fight our way out of jams.

One such situation occurred when we were picked up by the local sheriff in Fort Worth. He had quite a little scam going for himself there. He was paid probably two dollars a day per man to feed the prisoners in his Tarrant County Jail but would spend only about twenty cents a day for each man. But, of course, he was paid for each prisoner he housed in the jail, so it was important to him to keep the jail filled to capacity.

The typical sentence for vagrancy or for trespassing on railroad property was fifteen days' confinement. The police sweeps always netted five or six men and whenever a group of vagabonds had completed their sentence the sheriff would send his men out to round up another bunch to fill the vacancies.

We were all kept in one large "bull pen" that held about fifteen bunks. But there were always between thirty-five and forty men kept jammed in there. There was a pile of thin mattresses stacked up in one corner and each night those without a bunk had to grab one, stretch it out on the floor and sleep there. The accommodations were, to say the least, something less than lavish and the crowded conditions led to constant bickering among the inmates.

J. L. and I were singled out once or twice by a few of the old-timers who mistakenly believed that we were easy pickings for bullying and for sexual harassment. But, as I indicated, I was plenty strong, and so was Jimmy Lester. Either of us could whip a man, and the two of us could easily have killed a man. We never did kill anyone, but we sure knocked the hell out of several attackers. We were soon given a wide berth and actually got to be friends with some of the toughs.

There were a couple of cowboys in the jail when J. L. and I first arrived. They had been sentenced for fighting, I think. Since they seemed to have been there for a while and appeared to know their way around, I engaged one of them in conversation.

"What do they feed ya in here?" I asked him.

"Well," he replied, "for breakfast ya get oatmeal, for dinner ya get cornmeal and for supper ya get nomeal."

We soon found out that he hadn't been kidding. At breakfast, the guards came around with a large dishpan full of a thick, gummy substance, a mound of which they plopped on to a metal plate. The plate was then passed to a prisoner through a small opening in the bars. Each man got a plate of the goo and a cup of black coffee; there was no salt or sugar or milk provided to make it more palatable.

The breakfast meal, indeed, turned out to be oatmeal; at dinner (lunch) it was cornmeal and that evening we were indeed given "nomeal"—nothing!

The fifteen days dragged by painfully. Unlike the county or city jails farther north, this one didn't take us out on work gangs—the sheriff had no one in Fort Worth to whom he could merchandise his prison population; his profit came, instead, from the food allowance he received from Tarrant County. So we spent all of the time in the large pen. There was no exercise yard—our exercise came from the short but physically taxing fist fights J. L. and I were goaded into. Although I felt certain I could take care of myself, I was still glad J. L. was around.

After fifteen days of oatmeal, cornmeal and nomeal, we were released from Tarrant County jail. In Fort Worth, two dairy companies were waging a price war; ice cream was selling for ten cents a quart. Immediately, we each bought a quart.

That experience with the police was among the mildest we encountered during those two summers. This was at the height of the Depression; there were thousands of men riding freights and the railroad bulls were at the brutal peak of their power in the yards and on the trains.

• • •

There were bulls riding the trains in the 1930s and 1940s who, when they found men riding illegally, would make them jump off no matter how fast the train was going. Many men were being shot off the trains, their bodies buried alongside the tracks, their families never to know what had happened to them.

In the middle of Ohio there was a particularly vicious group of bulls led by a man called Lima Red. These bulls had carefully sharpened the front sight blades on their revolvers to a keen edge. When they caught men in the yards or on a train they would pistol-whip them, slashing their faces down to the bone. I've seen men whose cheeks were sliced so deep, you could see their jaws and their teeth through the wounds.

In Wyoming, two bulls decided they weren't catching enough men in the yards. On their own time they began riding the trains to Salt Lake City and back. Ranchers along a desolate stretch of the right-of-way began finding bodies almost weekly. Each had been killed with a bullet to the head.

In Chicago, four old men arrived on a freight in near-zero weather. They entered a yard shack to get warm and were discovered by a pair of railroad police who doused the old men with cold water and forced them back into the yard. Three died of exposure before they could escape. The bulls were tried and convicted for their murder.

Men on the road in those days had not only the railroad bulls and the local sheriffs to worry about. They were often set upon by young toughs who beat them up because they were strangers in town. In El Paso, Texas, a number of hobos, bums and winos were killed in a railroad yard just after they had left a nearby rescue mission. It was later learned that the killer was not connected with the railroad but was a demented individual who had murdered the innocent, unarmed men "just for the fun of it."

I learned, over the years, that some of the most vicious bulls received their own punishment. One case that I particularly remember was that of a bull in the Midwest who was known for his depraved treatment of hobos and other men of the road. One of his victims decided that he would exact revenge for the treatment he and a number of his friends had received at the bull's hands. One dark night, he crept into an empty boxcar which was sitting on a siding and waited for the bull to make his usual rounds. With the door open only a few feet, the 'bo hid in the shadows and, as he heard the bull approaching, began to moan as though he were ill. When the bull stuck his head in the boxcar door, the 'bo slid the heavy door shut on the bull's neck, breaking it and killing him instantly. This deadly retribution was not an unusual one in those hard, pitiless times.

It should not be inferred from the incidents described here that *all* railroad cops were sadistic brutes or that *all* local police were inhuman slave traders or that a great number of private citizens were unfriendly or cruel. During my years on the road I found many cops to be sensitive and understanding even while being reasonably firm in performing their duties; I found many local police to be charitable and helpful; and without the patience and generosity of the general population, a hobo could not have survived on the road.

There were many railroad cops—especially in the later years I traveled—who looked the other way in order to allow me to ride the freights. And until recent years, it was a common practice for a hobo, finding himself out on a cold or rainy night with no boxcar to crawl into or no jungle hut to give him shelter, to go to the local jail and ask to spend the night in one of the cells. The request was almost always granted and a warm breakfast was frequently provided to boot. And many a kindly housewife over the years gave a hungry caller at her back door food that she could not easily afford to give away.

. . .

During the winters of 1932 and 1933, I made pocket money working with my dad in his window-washing business and also worked for my sister Lulu.

When mother decided to go to live with her parents in Idaho, Lulu, who was then fifteen, rebelled. She didn't want to go West. Instead, she ran away, hitchhiking to Toledo to join our father. But Lu didn't like Dad's new family any more than I did when I was sent to live with him later. Less than a year after arriving, Lu got married and moved out of Dad's house.

She married a prohibition gangster, a member of the notorious Purple Gang of Detroit, a blood-thirsty, rum-running bunch that had frightened Al Capone's mob out of town when they attempted to set up operations in the Motor City.

In 1931, Lu's husband was arrested, tried and convicted for violations of the Volstead Act. He was sentenced to prison, leaving Lu to take over his "booze" operation in Toledo. She turned it into the biggest bootlegging operation in town. She owned several second-floor apartments located over storefronts in the near-downtown area. These apartments were used to store five-gallon cans of raw alcohol, which she sold to out-of-town buyers. Jimmy Lester and I worked part-time for Lu, loading and unloading the alcohol.

Soft-hearted Lu was a real easy touch. Whenever mobsters in Toledo got in trouble, they came to her and she was always ready to help them out with money or advice. The prostitutes in town knew her and when they were down on their luck and needed money, Lu was there to give it to them. I once calculated that she had given away over a million dollars. Yet when she died, there wasn't enough left to pay for her tombstone.

Because neither of us felt welcome among Dad's new

family, we had a close bond between us that lasted all her life. I was five years younger than she and even when I was a grown man with a family of my own, she still thought of me as her little brother.

When Jimmy Lester decided to join his family in Tennessee in 1934, I lost my dear traveling companion. And with my mother dead and my sister Alice starting her own family and a new life, I had little cause to go back to Idaho. It just wasn't the same back there; one of my Indian cousins had been killed, another had gone blind and the third had moved with his family to Washington state.

My life was changing, too. I was about to sever my connections with my father and go into the world totally on my own. While I had been initiated into one of the Brotherhood of the 'Bo clans, I still didn't consider myself a full-fledged hobo—that would come later.

CHAPTER 7
THE WAY OUT OF TOWN

In June 1934 I completed my sophomore year at Toledo's Libbey High School. I had made quite a name for myself in amateur wrestling. I'd won the city championship five years straight and had even been thrown into a couple of demonstration matches that didn't count for anything. But in one of them I beat the Ohio State University Big Ten champ, which embarrassed the hell out of him and the university.

Because of my wrestling prowess, I had been promised a full athletic scholarship to Ohio State University. But during my last term in high school my grades began dropping. I had missed a great deal of school, not because I was ill, but because of my very unpleasant home life.

My father was a very caring and generous man who became almost totally wrapped up in his new family, giving his stepchildren, all of whom were by now lazy, shiftless adults, just about anything they asked for. And yet he neglected to provide me with decent school clothes. The house was crowded with his second wife's children and itinerant relatives who always seemed to be showing up for a few days or a few weeks or even longer.

I thoroughly despised my stepmother's sons. They were a wild, undisciplined bunch who spent every night drinking and raising hell in the house. They were filthy and smelled bad, a condition that was completely unnecessary. It became impossible for me to study in this atmosphere and my relationship with them grew increasingly hostile. Finally, it erupted in a violent scene.

One of the sons, in his thirties, had been particularly offensive to me; he delighted in taunting me, teasing me and generally making my life miserable. He became so obnoxious one night that I couldn't take it any longer. I exploded, beating the hell out of him and actually chasing him into a bedroom and dragging him out from under a bed where he'd crawled trying to escape me. My stepmother was screaming wildly, convinced I was going to kill her son. And I might well have, if Dad hadn't finally come in and pulled me away from him.

This incident was the final blow for me. I decided I had to get out of there, to get as far away from them as I could.

When school was out for the summer I took off as usual. But this time I knew I was not coming back—at least not coming back to the way things had been. I wanted to stay in school, and I wanted to go on to college. But at that time I firmly believed that I had no other choice than to go on the road permanently.

Dropping out of school was a difficult decision for me, and there were many times during the next year when I regretted having made that choice. On cold, dark days when I was out of work and had no money, when there was no place to get in out of the rain and snow, I found myself thinking that perhaps I should go back. But I never seriously considered doing that. To begin with, I would have to repeat the tenth grade; I would be a full year behind. Then, too, I would have to move back in with my father's family, and that was totally unacceptable for me. Although I returned to Toledo many times in the following two years, I never stayed at Dad's place. Instead, I found a room somewhere or stayed with friends. I had completely burned my bridges as far as my father and his family were concerned. I still loved him and let him know occasionally that I was all right, but I could never allow myself to reenter that unpleasant environment.

I've often thought of my stepmother, and in later years came to realize that she had done her best with me. But she had her own children to consider and, perhaps rightly, their interests came first in her mind. I respect her for that, but my life might have been far different if I had been made to feel that I was genuinely wanted as a part of that family. It's quite possible that I would have gone into medicine; a dozen or more cousins, aunts and uncles had become doctors or nurses.

Jimmy Lester left Toledo with me, although it was understood that he would not spend the full summer on the road but would join his family later, after they had moved back to Tennessee. We spent the first month or two just hoboing around, seeing some more of the country. After he left me, somewhere in Texas, I continued roaming the countryside, learning more about the hobo life.

I discovered that many hobos were great naturalists who knew how to supplement their diets with the many herbs, edible weeds, roots, barks, mushrooms, berries, natural grains and nuts that were available to those who knew where to look and what to look for. They also knew how to hunt and trap silently and how to cook wild game as well as domestic animals.

Many 'bos were excellent outdoor chefs; there's a great difference between cooking in a well-equipped kitchen and over an open fire in the woods or along a riverbank. Hunters often hired hobos to go on their trips to cook for them. You couldn't find a better man to make you comfortable in the woods. He could always find a few things along a riverbank or forest trail to enhance a meal.

Whoever first said, "The best things in life are free," must have spent a lot of time in the woods and fields. In nature there is an abundance of nutritious, delicious foods growing wild. Such edibles are all around and most of us are totally unaware of the value of the growing things under our feet.

The American Indian was able to survive through many a cruel, harsh time because of his knowledge of the valuable foods in the wilds. Both from a medical and a culinary standpoint, the leaves, roots, bark and skin of literally thousands of plants in every part of this country grow unattended and waiting for us to use.

The common cattail has been called the "supermarket of the swamps." No plant, wild or domesticated, produces a greater variety of food than does the cattail. In the early spring, the young shoots can be pulled from the ground and peeled. The tender core can be cooked or eaten raw. In May or June, the green spikes can be cooked like any fresh vegetable. When the cattail starts to bloom, a yellow pollen is formed that has the consistency of fine-ground flour. It makes a most nourishing addition to pancakes or muffins. The rootstock can be dug up in early winter and ground or crushed into an excellent all-purpose flour. The dormant sprouts of next year's cattail can be eaten as a salad or cooked as a vegetable. At the juncture of the rootstock and the sprouts is a starchy core that can be roasted, boiled or cooked with a meat dish.

The leaves of many wild plants make tasty, healthful salads and cooked greens. Among these are the dandelion, peppergrass, purslane, pokeweed and watercress. Among the thousands of other edible plants growing in the wild are pigweed (also known as lamb's quarters, goosefoot or wild spinach) burdock, wild shallot, wild mustard, acorns, arrowhead, milkweed, velvet dock, red clover and calamus.

There are any number of others, so many, in fact, that a number of excellent books have been written about the variety, location, and methods of preparing these wild, no-cost delights. The late naturalist Euell Gibbons wrote several.

As with any domestic vegetable, timing is essential in harvesting and using wild plants. Many people have complained that they tried dandelion greens and didn't like the taste. Dandelions must be picked when they are young, tender and mild. At this stage they make a most delightful, delicious salad. The same is true with most other greens.

The roots of most wild plants may be used any time of year to make herbal medicines and teas, baking flours, and a number of other dietary uses. Chicory, soy bean and dandelion roots can be used to produce a very acceptable coffee substitute.

High-quality, delicious meat and fish dishes also used to be available to the hobo at no cost and with just a little effort. Box traps could be found near almost every hobo jungle during the 1930s. Hobos never used snares or leg traps. The box trap was a simple device with a sliding door that would fall shut when the game ventured inside to take the bait left there. Among the many types of game that hobos found in the wild were pheasant, quail, raccoon, possum, pigeon, muskrat and groundhog. And, of course, rabbit and squirrel also made savory meat courses for the hobos' dinner.

• • •

The number of transients found riding freights began to thin considerably in the mid-1930s as jobs began opening up. But the hobos continued undiminished. They weren't looking for jobs; they had no desire to settle down. The road was their life, their home, and I soon realized that it was my life and my home as well. I was no longer traveling just to get back to Idaho to see my sister or my friends, I was on the road because I couldn't stand to be tied down to one place very long.

During the years in which many transients were on the road, hobos tended to rely heavily on the branch lines—the short-distance lines that ran between towns—in order to make their "circuits," rather than the mainlines, which the transients preferred to get from one end of the country to the other. The transients rode the "high iron," so named because the rails on the mainline were made an inch or two higher than the branch lines to take the increased speed and heavier loads.

The dangers found riding the rails continued, the bad bulls were just as mean and the forced recruitment of work gangs did not slacken. Over the next couple of years I found myself captured by slave-hunting sheriffs many times. And each time I managed to make a speedy escape as soon as an opportunity presented itself.

I was proud and very pleased, during those years, to have been so well taught by the old hobos I met. Many of the would-be hobos I saw, those who had suddenly decided that it would be fun to "go on the bum" but had no training beforehand, fell victim to the perils of riding the trains. Uncounted numbers were seriously injured every year falling from boxcars, being caught under train wheels, leaving arms and legs severed, heads crushed. What I found almost a natural act in boarding a moving freight car proved deadly to those who had not been taught the proper way to accomplish this.

It was a pitiful sight to see a young, otherwise healthy teenager limping along on a pair of crutches with one pant leg hanging empty, or waving an arm with a stump where his hand should have been.

The attitude of many people, particularly in the smaller towns, continued to be anti-wanderer. Men of the road were not welcome in many communities across the country. The hobo had to learn which towns were safe for him to enter. At least one of the American states was strongly against anyone who even resembled a tramp or hobo or transient. The California State Police stationed troopers at the state line to pull men from freight cars and usher them back over the line, telling them that they should get jobs and come back to their state "like a man."

Since I was now hoboing full time, rather than riding to and from Idaho, I had a better opportunity to observe the life and activities of the hobos in much greater detail and I learned a good deal more about them than I had discovered in my previous years of summer travel.

I had been recruited as a member of the Brotherhood of the 'Bos at a very early age, far younger than most were allowed in. The reason, I discovered, was that the older 'bos, realizing that their time was limited, wanted someone who could record and pass on their history to generations yet to come. Because I was young and had an intense interest in their stories, I had been selected as a hobo's historian.

The 'bos had always impressed me as a very mild-mannered and sympathetic group of honest, ethical men. But I found that, as with any family, there was an occasional black sheep, one who was dishonest or of poor character. When the others found such a person in their ranks they exercised extreme measures to deal with those who violated their rules.

One night I came into a hobo jungle just as a "kangaroo court" went into session. An errant hobo had been accused of treating a number of housewives in the area in a very insulting manner. Abusive conduct by a hobo to a housewife was a serious breach of the hobo's code, one that had a profound effect on all hobos traveling in that area. One bad 'bo could spoil things for the others for a year or more, and such infractions were never taken lightly. The punishment for violations of the code ranged from a good swift kick in the pants—and a warning to the offending 'bo to straighten up—to a severe beating that could put the man in the hospital.

At this, my first sight of hobo justice, the punishment

meted out was a solid right to the defendant's jaw to "get his attention," followed by a stern admonition to hit the road and to never come back to the area.

"You get just one chance, brother," the prostrate man was told as he massaged his aching jaw. "You get out of this district and don't come back. If any of us catches you around here again, we'll kill ya."

I would observe a great many such "trials" over the years and would, myself, participate as a member of the jury in a number of them.

It was difficult to police the men on the road during the years when large numbers of transients were traveling the country. But the hobo did everything possible to insure that his relationship with townspeople was kept as smooth and uncomplicated as he could manage. It was crucial that housewives, particularly, maintain their image of the hobo as a "gentleman of the road." His survival depended on being able to call at the back door of a house and offer his labors in exchange for a meal.

The hobo code against thievery was strict but did have three minor loopholes. The first concerned fresh-baked pies. In the 1930s, housewives did almost all their own baking. When they baked pies they never limited the production to one or even two pies. Instead they usually baked three or four at a time, leaving them on the back porch to cool. There was an unwritten understanding between the hobo and the housewife that one of the pies was there for him; he didn't have to ask or even indicate to her that he was taking it. In one sense it provided a source of pride to the woman, making her feel that her baking skills were good enough to satisfy the hobo gourmet. But no matter how excellent the pies looked or smelled, the hobo would never take more than the one that had been left for him. Neither he nor the housewife considered this act stealing.

The same held true with milk from a farmer's cow. The hobo, in need of milk for his own cooking kettle, would often approach a cow grazing in the field, have a friend hold its head while he appropriated a single quart of milk. He never took more than the single quart and the farmer rarely objected.

One other example of the unique relationship the hobo had with many of the housewives in America concerned laundry—clean as well as soiled.

Each Monday morning—the traditional washday in the 1930s and 1940s—a hobo passing through town would scout the backyards of homes in the area. The drying clothes would be hanging on clotheslines everywhere. Under his arm, the hobo carried a bundle consisting usually of two shirts, two pairs of long underwear and several pairs of socks. The hobo was looking for men's clothing that appeared to be the same size as his own. Finding them, the hobo would lay his bundle of soiled shirts, underwear and stockings beneath the clothesline and exchange them for an equal quantity of the clean apparel hanging there. The goods left were always of equal or better quality and value as those taken. The housewives were not necessarily pleased with this unauthorized trade, but it was mutually understood that no theft had taken place. Such an affront would hardly be tolerated today—in those rare households where the wash is still hung in the sun to dry—but it was a common practice fifty years ago.

A hobo could always tell which homes were the best to call at; 'bos who'd been there ahead of him would leave signals and signs as to which places were good for a meal and which weren't. It might be a tree branch in front of the house bent at a certain angle and fastened with a rubber band or a piece of string. After several months the rubber band or the string would rot away but the branch would remain as a permanent sign to the hobo. Also, there were "hobo marks" which were chalked on walls and water towers and bridges to inform the traveler of the reception he could expect in the general area. These marks were somewhat complex and only the experienced hobo was usually able to decipher them.

A crude sketch of a pair of shovels indicated that an offer to work would get you a meal; a group of five or six circles indicated a good chance of some money being given there; the letter "T" leaning at an angle meant "get out of here fast." A square with a dot in the center chalked on the fence or sidewalk in front of a house told the hobo that "people who live here may treat hobos violently." And a rectangle with wavy lines inside meant "owner of this house has a bad temper," while the drawing of a crude bench told the 'bo that "sit-down meals are given to hobos here." An "X" with a head above it meant that a doctor gave hobos free medical treatment.

There were many such coded signs left in towns everywhere, and an experienced hobo was constantly on the lookout for them; they made his travels far easier. Of course, when no marks were present, the hobo who knew what to expect in the area contributed his knowledge for those who would come after him.

My work-for-hire, once I went on the road full time, was not limited to doing chores to survive. During the previous winter I had found some part-time jobs working in construction—mostly in brick masonry—at several Toledo petroleum refineries, and I realized I would be able to make more money doing this than working the harvests. But it was back-breaking labor; I had to carry a "hod" with between sixty and seventy pounds of bricks up ladders to where the men were laying them. I alternated the bricks with fifty-pound loads of mortar, which I had learned to mix.

The advantage of this kind of work was that jobs for cement masons paid better than following harvests and I could find jobs all year and just about everywhere in the country. It was a trade that would sustain me throughout my working life.

I continued riding trains, but slowly I switched from being a pure wandering hobo to a working hobo, or "boomer."

Having a trade to follow made life on the road a good

deal more comfortable. With money in my pockets I was assured of a good meal and a room if the weather was too disagreeable. Some of the time, after finishing a job at one location, I would hobo around, not necessarily looking for work. I would buy a chunk of meat and take it down to a hobo jungle and share it with the 'bos I found there. It always came as a pleasant surprise to them and I made many friends among the hobos with just this simple act of sharing my good fortune.

There were occasions when I hadn't looked for work, or there were no jobs starting up, and I found myself out of cash. When this happened I was able to fall back on my experience as a hobo and call on friendly housewives for a meal in exchange for doing some chores.

But, even when I was reasonably "flush" with pocket money, I still suffered the same treatment from the bulls and the local cops as the other hobos. Often, when we weren't harassed by the law, we had to deal with some of the townsfolk who looked down their noses at the men of the road. It caused more than a few unwanted street brawls when they attempted to show us the way out of town.

I had always had an intense love for automobiles. I'd taken a high school course in auto mechanics and was able to do almost all of the necessary repair work on cars of that era. And as a "boomer" I was able, at times, to accumulate enough money to buy a car which, in the 1930s, meant as little as ten dollars for a battered old Ford or Chevy.

The first automobile I owned was a 1923 Jewett, a huge machine with large showcase windows. I was only fifteen at the time I bought it—paying a whopping fifty dollars for it. I had to do a lot of work on it to keep it running and it wasn't very dependable. But I was as proud as if it was brand-new.

Probably the most beautiful machine I owned back then was a bootlegger's car that had been impounded when the police arrested him for transporting booze. It was a 1932 Stutz Blackhawk four-door sedan, turned out the last year that the company made that model. It had a straight-eight, twin overhead cam engine with twin ignitions, two spark plugs for each cylinder and two electric fuel pumps. It had been in the police pound for almost three years when I heard about it. My sister Lu, who had her own connections with the police, was able to arrange for me to buy it for about $375.

It had huge tires and wheels with racing hubs and electric wire defrosters imbedded in the front windshield. It only got about six miles to the gallon and the tires were in bad shape, so I always left it in Toledo when I went on the road.

In January 1936, as I began what was to be my first year of full-time hoboing, I felt certain I had found the secret to true happiness and total freedom. I was accepted by the hobos as a *man* of the road, a kid no longer. I firmly considered myself one of them, a member of the Brotherhood of the 'Bo, no longer tied to a home base, but belonging to a neighborhood that stretched as far as the iron road I traveled, and having a family whose members could be found in every hobo jungle that dotted the trackside everywhere in the country.

CHAPTER 8

MAGPIES AND PETTICOAT BUMS

Along with the thousands of men wandering the country in the 1930s were hundreds of women, mostly transients following the harvests, largely homeless, usually alone and almost always as tough and hard as nails.

The abusive term "tramp," meaning an unsavory woman, found its way into the dictionary from those days when women traveled the road.

But rather than someone of loose morals, I found those with whom I came in contact to be solitary people who were riding the freights for the same reason many men were, to find work, trying to survive in an era when survival was a twenty-four-hour-a-day struggle, when starvation was an ever-present threat to countless thousands of unfortunate Americans.

There were, to be sure, exceptions. One such exception was Boxcar Bertha.

Bertha Thompson was born near the turn of the century near the Northern Railroad tracks in Kansas, the first of four children, all of whom were of different fathers. Her first playhouse was a boxcar and by the time she was twelve she had already hopped a freight and ridden to the next division and back. At fifteen she left home to ride the rails. Over the following fifteen years Bertha hoboed from one end of the country to the other, spent time as part of a gang of shoplifters, became a prostitute in a Chicago brothel and finally worked for a New York social bureau where she gathered statistical material on the numbers of women traveling the road during the Great Depression.

By 1937, in collaboration with Dr. Ben L. Reitman, she penned her autobiography, *Sister of the Road,* a well-written, entertaining and important work, and she deserves to be commended for her efforts. She made a worthwhile contribution to the hobo history. But Bertha was a dramatic exception to the female hobo rule. During my years on the iron road, most women were riding the trains just to get from one harvest to the other or to search for work or a better life.

Those who knew no better assumed that these women were "easy," immoral whores who, like the camp followers of Civil War days, were on the road because that's where the men were. The truth of the matter was, women who offered their bodies to men did so on the streets of cities and towns, where the "pickings" were far better than in the boxcars and in the hobo jungles of the country. The men of the road offered nothing of value to women; they had no money, and they could not provide security and comfort. There was little that hobos could possibly provide other than a share of their meager meals.

Almost certainly there were some women—the vulnerable ones—who experienced sexual assaults on the road.

But these were the rare exceptions; in my experience, I never knew of a woman being molested by a hobo.

The women would come into a jungle, usually alone. They would find a secluded spot on the fringes of the campfire, roll up in their blankets and keep to themselves throughout the night. They could sleep in a hobo jungle or in a boxcar with other hobos and never be bothered.

I saw many single women who were on the road for years, traveling on the same trains as 'bos but never *with* them. If you engaged one in conversation they would respond courteously but never warmly; they didn't encourage your approach. They were frequently as cold as steel but only as a protective measure—not necessarily out of a dislike for other people. They knew that as long as they stayed close to the hobos they would be safe. Still, they seldom wanted to be a part of the group.

The older hobos tended to resent the "magpies" or "petticoat bums," feeling that a woman shouldn't be on the road. But they tolerated them and extended their protection to them.

The women were excellent workers; they could keep up with the men in the fields and they could pick more fruit than most men could.

During the Depression, many women chose to go on the road with their men. I recall seeing many such families: the husband, his wife and one or more children, all riding on freights, staying in hobo jungles and working in the fields with other hobos and transients. It was a particularly sad picture; a family driven by desperation, roaming the country hoping to find an opportunity for a secure, happy future. For years, it was a futile search. The women who traveled alone were also searching, often unsure exactly what they were searching for, other than a peace of mind that many would never find.

Later, in the mid-1960s, women again took to the road in large numbers, again unsure of why. They were, for the most part, cast from a different mold than those who wandered during the Depression years. There was a far different moral climate in the 1960s, and drugs played a prominent role.

However, among those on the road during the sixth decade of the twentieth century there were a few who more aptly fit the mold of exceptional women like Boxcar Bertha. Among them was Luann Uhden, who called herself Lu the Lush, and Liz Williams, also known as Hobo Liz Lump (I believe that Liz was the only black woman ever to be elected Hobo Queen). And I met other unusual women wayfarers in the 1970s and 1980s, traveling alone through the United States. Some were bicycling around the country and at least one was hiking through the Sahara Desert. Another, K.C. Pace, cared for an ill husband until he died and then, in her sixties, went on the road, learned to fly an airplane and traveled around the world. She spent some of that time living in the Tibetan Himalayas.

And there have been many women who joined their husbands—retired or "reformed" hobos—traveling around the country, enjoying the thrill of life in the open, of riding freight trains and living in the few hobo jungles that survived until the late 1960s.

Another minority among those on the road were blacks. Although there were many blacks traveling in the Depression years, looking for work, searching for a future, not many sought membership in the hobo brotherhood.

But I had occasion to meet and get to know many blacks who were wandering, men like Double Portion who got his name because of his habit in a food line of always ordering twice as much as the man ahead of him. And there was a man who, when I met him, had no road name. After I got to know him I gave him the name "Shadow," which he liked and adopted as his own.

Black wanderers were largely accepted by the other hobos I knew. There were instances—particularly in the South—where black men were not allowed to ride in the same boxcar with whites. "This car is full, find one farther down the line," was a common rejection they faced. But the men who would not ride with a black were mostly the bums and the winos. By and large, white hobos were willing to accept and share a freight car or their meager meals with blacks as readily as with anyone else. "I don't care what a man looks like on the outside," an old brother once told me. "I'm interested in how he is on the inside."

Prejudice, discrimination and racism were a part of the world the hobo was trying to escape; having experienced the intolerance of those who despised hobos, the 'bo tended to make the acceptance of others—no matter what their color—a legacy that they hoped would be passed on to everyone. I'm proud to have helped to spread the hobo legacy.

CHAPTER 9

GET YERSELF A WIDDER WOMAN

The hobo, in spite of his nomadic life, often had "romantic" attachments to fulfill his carnal needs. Since he usually traveled in a circuit, around a fixed territory, it was possible to make acquaintance with a number of women without men of their own.

"Get yerself a widder woman" was a frequent bit of advice older 'bos gave younger ones when the question of how the new recruit would spend the coming winter. Finding an agreeable "widder" could mean the difference between heading for a warmer climate when the icy winds began to blow and settling in some cozy home to await the springtime, taking care of the place, doing chores and in general being helpful to the lonely lady as well as providing companionship.

Sometimes the wintering hobo would find a job in the town where he stayed, and often he would be a temporary "househusband," getting up to make the fire, doing the cooking, caring for his hostess when she was ill and in general trying to make her life more comfortable, more enjoyable during his stay.

Of course, not all of the hospitable women were widows. Many, if not most, were unmarried middle-aged females who were not concerned about any town gossip that might result from a stranger suddenly moving in with the local spinster.

I knew many hobos who wintered up with a "schoolmarm" or a "widder." They felt it was easier than heading for the Gulf Coast, although it did present certain problems. Usually the woman expected the 'bo to stick around when the snow melted and would put up quite a fuss when he began packing his bindle. But quite often, when he returned to town the following winter, he was invited back in.

In some of the larger cities there were kindly rooming-house-owning women who took pity on the 'bos and always made at least one of their empty rooms available to them. This was not done out of any romantic attachment the women felt toward homeless hobos, but rather out of a sense of Christian charity. The women were almost always known by the hobos as "mother" or "aunt" someone or other.

I've even heard of infrequent incidents where chorus girls or burlesque dancers and strippers have taken a hobo in for the winter.

Early in my hobo career, I had my own experience being sheltered by a woman, although this one was far from being either a widow or a schoolmarm.

In 1937, I was in Port Arthur, Texas, looking for construction work. I'd spent time that year working in the west Texas oil fields and refineries. While I was there, I ran into a friend from Toledo named Jack Hartman. Jack had heard that a Pure Oil refinery was to be built in Muskogee, Oklahoma, about 800 miles north. Another friend, whose full name I have forgotten but who was called Shorty, also planned to head for Muskogee. Shorty had a 1927 Studebaker President, a huge eight-cylinder machine that ate gasoline by the gulp. He wanted to take the car with him and invited Jack and me to drive north with him. I suggested that we ride the freights but the two argued against it and I finally agreed to go along in the car.

The problem with taking the automobile was that, while gasoline was only seventeen cents a gallon back then, none of us had any money. As one who had been carefully instructed by the hobos in the importance of strict honesty, I found it very difficult to become a party to what we had to do to travel the distance between Port Arthur and Muskogee: we stole gas all along the route, usually from parked trucks and highway construction sites.

Muskogee, a small town in those days, was jammed to the rafters with men seeking work at the refinery site. The three of us were able to secure employment with no trouble, but then we had the problem of where to stay until we received our first paycheck, which wouldn't come for about two weeks. We were told that every available bed in town had been taken; men were sleeping in alleys and cars and in empty buildings. You couldn't rent a cot in town no matter how much money you had, we were informed.

I had my bedroll with me and some cooking utensils; I could have lived outside while I was waiting for money and I might have been able to get a meal at least once a day by calling at someone's back door. But it would have been a considerable hardship after a long day's work, and I also had the other two to think about; they weren't prepared for that ordeal. Since I had experience in managing under all kinds of circumstances on the road, I was determined that I would somehow rustle up a place to sleep. And before too long I came upon—of all things—the White Elephant Hotel, a huge, white building three stories high down by the railroad depot.

We went inside and I confronted the manager, a beautiful Indian woman, a supremely tough gal with cold black eyes that at times flashed fire. She was tough as iron and carried a .45 caliber pistol hidden under her dress between her breasts.

When I asked about rooms for me and my two pals, she laughed and explained that the White Elephant Hotel was not a hotel any longer.

"This is a cathouse," she explained. "I just rent rooms for an hour at a time."

She had twenty women working for her, who, I noticed, were sitting in the lobby, listening to the radio and rapping on the front windows to attract potential customers passing by on the street.

Anyone else finding himself under these circumstances would probably have considered the situation hopeless and would have beat a hasty retreat feeling foolish and embarrassed. But I was desperate and my hobo experiences had made me accustomed to sweet-talking a woman. So I showed her our work tickets, proving that we did, indeed, have jobs to go to.

"M'am, we just got jobs here and we need a place to lie down. I though you might have a room we could use. We don't have a dime between us and it'll be two weeks before we get paid. As a matter of fact, I don't know how we're gonna eat until we get paid. But if you could help us out, we'll pay you back whatever you ask."

She looked long and hard at me and asked how old I was; I told her, twenty. I could tell from the way she was looking me over that she was thinking, "Still wet behind the ears." Finally she said:

"I feel sorry for you boys; I'm going to help you."

She took us up to the third floor, which was an attic/

storage area. The place was hot and dusty and dirty. But there were a number of beds with stained mattresses scattered around.

"Clean this place up and set up three beds," she ordered. "I'll get you sheets and pillow slips."

After about an hour she returned and inspected the place. Nodding her approval, she signaled us to return to the first floor with her. Once there, she led us across the street to a restaurant where she bought and gave us three meal tickets. The tickets had dollar and cent boxes around the edges that totaled ten dollars. Each time the holder bought a meal, the cashier would punch out the amount on the ticket. The ten dollars would feed us handsomely for two weeks: a good steak, beans and a salad cost less than a dollar; a hearty breakfast cost only thirty or thirty-five cents.

Back at the White Elephant our benefactress laid down a few commandments that we would have to obey while staying under her roof:

"You can come downstairs and sit in the lobby where the girls are and read the papers or listen to the radio. But you won't lay a hand on any of them or fraternize with them. And you're not allowed up in any of the 'work rooms.' You're too young. And if you ever come in drunk or if you ever bring anyone with you, I'll throw you out."

"We'll be good," I promised.

When we got our first paychecks we paid her for the meal tickets and the small amount she agreed on for the room. But because rooms were still impossible to find in town, she allowed us to stay, and we remained at the cathouse for over three months. Only on one occasion did we violate her rules, and that one time had violent repercussions.

On our first payday we were feeling flush. The job we were on paid eighty-five cents an hour—good money for those days—which meant that even after paying the White Elephant's madam and buying our own meal tickets, we still had more than a hundred dollars between us, and we wanted some action.

We'd gone uptown and visited a couple of saloons. In one place we met three men who said they were looking to shoot craps, but the police were everywhere and were hauling guys in for gambling. It was about eleven at night, and we knew the White Elephant would be busy and going strong. Thinking that our landlady would be fully occupied moving customers in and out and wouldn't be paying too much attention to what we might be doing, we decided we would take the three men back to our room.

There was an outside staircase leading to the third floor and, after warning the trio to be very quiet, we smuggled them upstairs. We spread a blanket on the floor and began our crap game.

Gilbert, Shorty and I were streetwise, we thought, and believed we could handle any hustlers. So we positioned ourselves between each of the other three to prevent them from passing loaded dice back and forth. It became apparent that they were "yeggs," a road name for crooks, and were trying to cheat, but we stymied them every time. Finally, when we had taken their entire roll of about a hundred bucks, they became very belligerent and demanded their money back. We refused and they left saying that they were going out to get more money.

A little later they returned, again demanding the money we'd taken from them. When we again refused, one of the three drew a pistol and ordered us to hand over the money.

But when they'd come back up the outside stairway, our landlady had heard them. The men were standing in the center of the room with the gun leveled at us when she burst through the door with her .45 drawn.

She shot one round into the ceiling and shouted at the three:

"Get out of here right now, and if any of you come back, I'll kill you."

The trio left hurriedly, speeding down the stairs. In fact, they were in such a hurry that one of them stumbled and fell just as she fired another shot in the air. The other two thought their confederate had been shot and let out some terrible screams. But they all kept going when they reached the ground and we never saw them afterwards.

After they'd gone, I was certain that we'd be sent packing as well. Instead, our generous madam gave us an all-time chewing out, waving her pistol in the air and making me fear that she would end up shooting the bunch of us.

"I trusted you, took you under my wing, fed you," she shouted. "Those men could have killed you, even if you gave their money back. Now, I like you boys and I'm still goin' to take care of you. But if you ever pull a trick like this again, I'll shoot you in the leg!"

"M'am, we promise we'll never do that again," I replied with all the seriousness I could muster. And we never did.

When the job was finished, we said our emotional goodbyes to this soft-hearted woman who had been so good to us, promising never to forget her or her kindness. And we never did, either.

Steam Train Maury Graham in a 1973 portrait taken soon after his election as National King of the Hobos. *(From the author's collection.)*

A pair of 'bos. Tarrant County District Attorney Doug Crouch poses with Maury in front of the court house in Fort Worth, Texas. Crouch, known as Lonesome Whistle, hoboed through the southwest in his younger days, before enrolling in law school. Steam Train traveled to Fort Worth for this 1973 photo at the invitation of the D.A. *(From the author's collection.)*

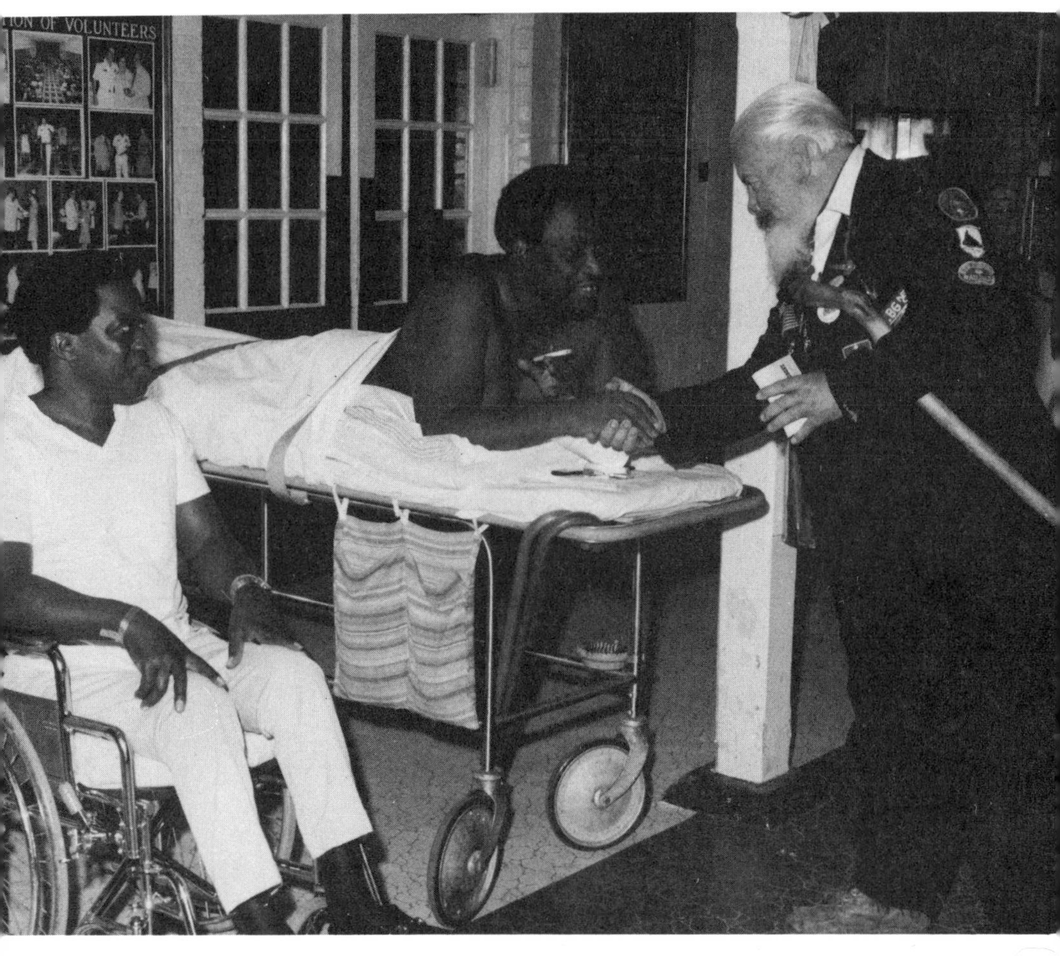

Richmond, Virginia was the scene of this VA hospital call, one of thirty-four thousand bedside visits Steam Train made in 1973–74. *(From the author's collection.)*

Children have always been among Steam Train's most avid fans. Here he poses with a school group in front of a restored railroad passenger car. *(From the author's collection.)*

"Howdy, pardner." Steam Train stops to shake the hand of two-year-old Todd Willhide at the Catoctin Colorfest in Thurmont, Maryland. Standing in the center is Thomas F. Barron, Sr., a police lieutenant with the Western Maryland Railway. *(Photo by Ann B. Love.)*

A study in pen and ink. Steam Train has been the subject of numerous drawings and paintings by the prison inmates he has visited. This one was done by Rick Sikes, while a prisoner at Leavenworth Federal Penitentiary. A talented country and western singer and composer as well as a capable artist, Sikes is now part owner of a small recording company in west Texas. Steam Train considers Sikes one of his "Friends for Life." *(Drawing courtesy of Rick Sikes.)*

A recent photo of the king shows Maury dressed in more informal road clothes. He still retains his battered hat and walking stick. *(From the author's collection.)*

The gov's friend. In this 1986 photo, Iowa Governor Terry E. Branstad presents Steam Train with a proclamation honoring his dedication to the annual Britt Hobo Convention. The governor is wearing the traditional red bandana, the symbol of hobos and railroad men. Also attending the ceremony was Jacqueline Day, former secretary to the governor and more recently chairman of the Britt Hobo Days Parade Board. *(From the author's collection.)*

Mayor Steam Train. Tom Griffith, mayor of Amory, Mississippi, presents Maury with a proclamation declaring him Honory Mayor of Amory during the annual railroad festival in 1980. Steam Train is an annual visitor to the festival each April. *(From the author's collection.)*

Dolly Parton takes time out of her busy concert schedule to pose with her friend Steam Train. *(From the author's collection.)*

CHAPTER 10

THE EARTH IS MY PILLOW

In the mid-1930s the petroleum boom in the U.S. was in full swing. The country was becoming more and more dependent on the automobile as a means of private transportation, and the use of coal as a residential heating fuel was rapidly being replaced by oil. Oil fields and refineries were springing up all over the country and particularly in Texas and Oklahoma, providing ready employment to those who had the necessary skills.

My experience in brick and cement work made it possible for me to find work for extended periods of time, often for as long as a year or more.

Being on my own with no real responsibilities other than to myself, I lived a happy, carefree life, working when I wanted, going on the road and traveling with the other hobos when I felt like it. Money wasn't the deciding factor governing when I sought work and when I hoboed. I could survive quite well with money or without it. I took jobs whenever the spirit moved me. If the job looked interesting or there was something—like a car—that I saw and wanted to buy, I went to work. When the job finally petered out—as they almost always did—I hit the road again, riding the freights until I found another job that attracted my attention.

Hoboing was a thoroughly natural thing for me by then. I knew just about all the tricks of the trade, I could always get a meal, I could always find a place to sleep and I could, if I wished, take advantage of one of the best government-sponsored assistance programs of that era: the Transit Bureau.

Found in most large cities, the Transit Bureau was designed to give Depression era assistance to men on the road or merchant mariners without a berth. Those in need could go to the Transit Bureau to find a good hot meal and lodging in clean, dry, warm dormitories provided with clean sheets and blankets.

Frequently men who came to the bureaus were able to find a place to work for a time. Those in charge would seek to find them temporary work in city parks, repairing streets, and other community projects. The jobs usually paid a dollar a day and a bag of Bull Durham tobacco. A man was only permitted to stay at the bureau for three days and then would have to move on, either to a local mission or to a "sally"—the hobos' term for the Salvation Army—or head to another city with a Transit Bureau.

Barbers, shoemakers, tailors and other craftsmen were welcome to stay as long as they wished and were paid two dollars a day and sometimes more. They were encouraged to stay in order to provide haircuts or shoe repairs and clothes cleaning and mending for the men who came for help. The facilities were clean, warm and well maintained and they were often a good deal better than the missions many retreated to when in need. The Transit Bureau would supply a desperate need in today's society.

Jimmy Lester OdNeal and I were in Galveston, Texas, in 1933 and went to their bureau while waiting for a job to turn up. They put us to work with several other residents moving beds and mattresses from the third floor to the basement. The staircases from the third floor ran in one continuous line all the way to the ground. The beds we were moving were single, or perhaps three-quarter beds, and we discovered that, rather than carry the heavy springs and the unwieldy mattresses down four flights of stairs, we could place the mattresses on the bedsprings and slide them down the stairs on the rounded metal frames that ran along the bottom of the springs. We quickly found that it was essential that we open the first floor door to the street and station one person outside to warn pedestrians away because the springs and mattresses built up terrific speed coming down the long stairway and came hurtling out the door and across the street like a shooting star. It was great fun to watch.

But one of the fellows working with us had a jug of wine that he began passing around. After a half dozen or so passes, Jimmy and I decided it would be a thrill to climb aboard the spring and mattress for a ride to the first floor. We both had just enough wine in us at the time to refuse to heed the advice of the others to not take the ride. Instead, we each climbed on a spring/mattress sled and pushed off, hanging on for dear life as the unguided missiles rocketed downward. I can only imagine what passersby must have thought as they witnessed two drunken fools flying out of the door and halfway across the street, skidding amid a shower of sparks while seated on a bedspring and mattress.

If there were no bureaus available to me, I still had the hobo jungles that I could seek out to share a meal and some friendly companionship with my "brothers." And even in the absence of a jungle, I had been so well schooled in outdoor living that I could easily get by until something better came along or I decided to go back to work.

In 1935, I found myself in Odessa, Texas, which was then just a tiny town of about 3,000 population. You could almost throw a rock from downtown to the city limits. It was a dreary place where the sand constantly blew down the main street, pushing rolling tumble weeds that would pile up in the doorways, requiring that you kick them out of the way before entering a shop or store and then hurry inside before the huge balls of dried vegetation could follow you in.

I had gone there to work in the new oil fields that were being drilled in the area. In spite of the frenzied oil exploration taking place, there seemed to be no rush to buy up the vacant land available. I was pestered for a time by a real estate salesman who pressured me to buy some property just outside of town. "You should get yourself some just to have it," he insisted. It was selling for ten dollars an acre and I seriously considered buying about five acres. I could then tell my friends back home that I owned a "Texas ranch." I finally decided against it, telling the salesman that the land "was worthless, even a rattlesnake couldn't make it out there in the blowing sand."

Needless to say, the area became one of the hottest oil fields the state of Texas ever knew. Oil was being found everywhere; they were drilling wells and finding oil all over town—they even drilled one in the middle of the town's high school football field—and the property I could have bought for fifty dollars would probably have made me a millionaire several times over.

But I was happy living an uncomplicated life. I had a room in a small boarding house and had even found myself a steady girl friend—a beautiful Mexican girl. I stuck around Odessa until there was no longer work for me and then I went back on the road.

Although I had taken the step toward total independence from my father and his family, I had not divorced myself from the city where most of my younger friends still lived. I traveled my own hobo circuit between Toledo and Texas, returning to Toledo periodically, working there for a time and then jumping on a freight and hitting the road again. In 1936 I took a job offered under the Depression recovery process, which had me teaching wrestling at two Toledo high schools for fifteen dollars a week.

I had a small room in the downtown section of Toledo which I shared with an old hobo I had met when I first began visiting the local jungle. His name was Sandusky Red and he was a fountain of hobo lore; I loved being around him. Years later I would wonder if he felt the same about me after a frightening incident we experienced while he lived with me.

There had been a notorious gangster running around the Midwest in 1936 and 1937 robbing banks and in general being a very unpleasant character. There had been photos of him in the local papers and posted in every police station and post office. I didn't notice it myself at the time, but my landlady decided that the resemblance between me and the crook was unmistakable.

One night, Red and I walked into our room, having just returned from bar-crawling, to find a virtual army of police and FBI agents with pistols and shotguns and machine guns, all shouting, "Yep, that's him, that's him," and waving the guns in my face and jabbing me in the ribs. "Don't move or we'll kill you."

I was dumbfounded, not to mention frightened out of my boots.

"What's the matter with you guys?" I said as they cuffed our hands behind our backs.

They showed me a picture of the gangster, insisting it was a photo of me.

"You're crazy," I said. "I'm not that guy, and I can prove it. My dad lives just up the street, you can ask him."

But they weren't convinced. I was now very frightened,

my knees were trembling. It was obvious that these men were serious; they believed they had captured a cold-blooded desperado and it was going to take something approaching a miracle to make them think otherwise. I was terrified that they might shoot me before I had a chance to prove who I really was. Then I noticed something in the profile picture of the bank robber.

"Look at his right ear," I demanded. "Look at it, it's normal. Now look at mine."

As a result of years of wrestling, I had developed a severely cauliflowered ear. It was undeniable proof that I was not the bank robber. After examining both the photo and my deformed ear, the police and FBI apologized and hastily left the apartment. The bank robber was killed in a shoot-out in Bangor, Maine, several months later, after he had robbed a hardware store of a number of guns.

I continued the teaching job until the end of the school year. I then bought a beat-up 1927 Chevy and teamed up with my old friend, Gilbert Fair, for a trip back to west Texas, where I'd heard there was more work in the oil fields.

The trip south was pleasant—the old car chugged smoothly along—until we got halfway through Texas. There we ran into an intense sandstorm that came roaring over the flatland in a huge black cloud that looked just like a tornado. The rumbling, churning cloud terrified both of us; we had no idea how serious it was or how to get out of its path. When it hit us it rolled us over into a ditch breaking out all the glass and springing the doors. Fortunately, neither of us was injured. Several men came along in another car and helped us roll my car back on its wheels. The old thing started right up but we had to tie the doors shut. I kept it for most of the year we worked down there and it continued to get us where we wanted to go, although we still had to tie the doors shut and, since I never replaced the broken windows, it was most uncomfortable when it rained.

We worked our way around west Texas, booming in the

fields at Kilgore, Big Spring and Monahans, and making periodic trips back to Toledo in between jobs.

I now had a very special reason for wanting to get back to Toledo. The reason was a lovely blue-eyed brunette named Wanda.

CHAPTER 11

TO GO HOBOING NO MORE

For the better part of six years I had been contented with the hobos as my "family." I was proud to have been accepted by them, to feel that wherever I went I could find the companionship I had so desperately longed for as a child.

But by 1936, a strange yearning for more than what my contact with other hobos could provide had begun intruding on what had seemed to be an idyllic life. I felt that something was missing, that perhaps the time had come when I should consider having a more traditional family.

While working in Toledo early in 1936, I met Wanda Matty, a lovely eighteen-year-old who worked in the dietary department of the Women's and Children's Hospital (later changed to Riverside Hospital) in the city.

She was born Wanda Marion Matyanczyk in a Polish neighborhood of Toledo called Lagrinka, one of the three daughters and five sons born to Felix and Lottie Matyanczyk. Her parents shortened the family name to Matty because spelling the old country name gave everyone fits.

Wanda was going with another fella at the time, but I was persistent and I finally talked her into breaking a date with the other guy to go out with me. We went with another couple to a nightclub and to a dance on that first date.

We began dating regularly and as the months passed it became increasingly apparent to me that Wanda was very, very special. She seemed to have the same adventuresome spirit that I considered important to my own life; she was very bright, soft-spoken when she had something to say and an excellent listener when I was talking —an important asset in a woman, I always believed.

We began to date each other exclusively. But after a few months, when work in Toledo slackened, I decided I had to go back on the road. But suddenly, the magic I'd always felt when heading out of town faded, the thrill of being free and able to wander whenever I wished was replaced with a longing to be again with the one person who had come to mean more to me than the open road.

Whenever I was away I kept in touch with Wanda through the mails, always happy to return to Ohio when a job was over. Early in 1937 I knew that I could never do better in finding a wife than the lovely, charmingly petite girl waiting for me in Toledo.

On May 11, 1937—Wanda's nineteenth birthday—we became engaged. I had been working again in Toledo, but soon after our engagement I had to leave town again for a job I thought was waiting for me in Port Arthur, Texas, then to Muskogee, Oklahoma, returning to Toledo at Christmas time. Then it was back to Texas again, continuing our letter-writing correspondence, which quickly proved totally unsatisfactory. By April of 1938 I had had enough loneliness. I wrote to Wanda, saying: "This is for the birds. I'm going to get you down here so we can get married." I sent money for busfare and on April 27 she arrived in Port Arthur. Oltha OdNeal, wife of Ed OdNeal —Jimmy Lester's brother—met her as I was still at work.

We had planned to marry on Wanda's twentieth birthday. But having her there was too much for me, I wanted her to be my bride as soon as possible. So on Saturday, April 30, 1938, Wanda Matty and Maurice Graham became man and wife.

I had never fully explained that I was a hobo. She knew that I traveled in search of work, but she wasn't totally aware of my years on the road or that sometimes I rode the freights simply for the freedom and the adventure and the pleasure of being on the move. But now I was a married man, planning to have a family. I realized that the old days, as sweet and satisfying as they were, would no longer be a proper life for me; I could no longer participate in the ways of the brotherhood. In taking unto myself a wife I had forsaken my life as a hobo.

I promised myself that I would be a conscientious husband and a member of the "home guard." For the next thirty-one years I would keep that promise.

If Wanda had dreams of a quiet, secure home where I would return each night, lunch pail in hand, she would, for the most part, be disappointed. Almost from the day we were married, we were on the move as one job ran out and another, in some different location, opened up. Nine times out of ten, when a job was finished there would be a month or more before the next one was scheduled to begin. During these slack periods Wanda and I returned to her mother's home in Toledo. When the job began, I would go down and look around for a suitable apartment before having Wanda join me. Not infrequently, she would pack all our belongings in our car and drive to wherever I was. These were long hard motor trips for a young woman driving all alone in a car subject to mechanical breakdowns and on narrow, often poorly maintained roads—there were no freeways or turnpikes in those days.

But we had an active, enjoyable life in the early days of our marriage. In the beginning, Wanda enjoyed the travel, seeing parts of the country she had never previously visited. And, in Texas, there were some people who thoroughly enjoyed having her there. The woman who ran a small neighborhood grocery near our rented apartment in Port Arthur thrilled whenever she saw Wanda come in; she was unaccustomed to northerners and delighted in hearing Wanda speak with her strange accent and peculiar use of words.

For her part, Wanda also found many differences in the people we met there. When we inspected what was to become our first apartment, Wanda noticed that the landlady made frequent trips to the kitchen sink to spit, and when we were in other rooms the woman carried a can with her in which she expectorated.

"Why did she have to spit like that?" Wanda asked me when we left the apartment.

I explained that a great many women in the south used snuff or chewing tobacco. Wanda was aghast and assured me that, regardless of what the women there did, *she* had no intention of succumbing to that local custom.

As a "boomer" I was moving from one job to another about every three to six months, traveling not unlike the way I had during the years I spent on the road—"rubber tire hobos" is about what we were then. But we were young and had no definite roots, no responsibilities to anyone but ourselves.

Then, on September 12, 1939, our lives changed dramatically; our first child, Alice Lou, was born in Toledo. From that time on traveling posed greater problems. But Wanda accepted the hardships without complaint and little Alice seemed to thrive on our nomadic life.

When World War II broke out I was helping to build army air bases and was granted a draft deferment as part of "essential industry." Then, as the Allies prepared for the invasion of Europe and the need for additional troops became critical, my deferment was withdrawn and I was ordered to report for induction. On January 11, 1944, just three weeks before I was scheduled to leave for Camp Atterbury, Indiana, our second child, Karen Suzanne was born. I was leaving a wife and two children behind and, like so many other men, embarking on an adventure the likes of which I had never expected to see. The uncertainty and the potential danger was not lost on me as I said my good-byes to my family, not knowing whether I would see them again or not.

After basic training I was assigned to the army engineers which, given my background in construction, seemed appropriate and sensible. But shortly thereafter I was reassigned to the medical detachment of the engineers. How my experience in cement masonry qualified me as a medic I couldn't understand, and I was given no opportunity to demand an explanation.

After a brief stay in England—during which I was able to travel to Scotland and trace my family tree—we were shipped out to the continent. My unit was sent into the liberated Nazi concentration and extermination camps to help treat what survivors remained. I saw firsthand the stacks of human bodies piled like cordwood awaiting the bulldozer's push into huge burial pits filled with lime. It was a vision that haunts me still, an experience that demonstrated, more than any of the examples of brutality and inhuman conduct that I had witnessed on the road, how perverted the human soul can become.

My years as a hobo had prepared me extremely well for the life of a soldier. Unlike most of the hobos before me, who had learned their outdoor skills during military service and then brought them back with them to civilian life, I had developed the skills first and then took them into my army service. Therefore, I was able to adapt readily to the discomforts of living in the field, and the self-reliance and ingenuity I had learned from the hobos served me very well on several occasions.

Having heard a great many rumors about our imminent reassignment to the Pacific theater, I decided to take a short furlough to see a bit more of Europe before we were shipped out. To my surprise I found on my return to the camp that, while I was away, the unit had been suddenly ordered to Marseilles for shipment to the Pacific where we were to take part in the invasion of the Japanese home islands.

"How am I supposed to get to Marseilles?" I asked the officer who had been left behind with a small contingent to close the camp.

"That's your problem, soldier," he replied. "But you'd better find a way to get there, otherwise you'll be AWOL."

There was no available transportation, either civilian or military, and I was several hundred miles away. Then I remembered that, while there was no widespread passenger service, much of the railroad freight system had been restored to ship needed food and other supplies throughout the war-torn country. It took a bit to learn from French railroad dispatchers which lines were running and which trains were going south, but, finally, I was able to use my hobo talents to ride the rails and to reach the seaport in plenty of time to board the troopship with my unit.

About two weeks later, as we were nearing the Panama Canal, our ship suddenly swung wildly to one side in an extremely sharp turn. Those of us on deck assumed that the ship was taking evasive action against a submarine attack, although we were puzzled as to who was attacking; the war with Germany had long since concluded and it seemed most unlikely that a Jap sub would be operating in this part of the world.

As we watched the wake of the ship in the turn, the public address system came to life and an excited voice announced that the Japanese had just surrendered: the war was over! The voice continued that the troop vessel ahead of us had just passed through the Canal and was ordered to continue on to Japan to take part in the occupation of that country. But, since we had not yet reached Panama, our orders were to proceed to Norfolk, Virginia, where we would be mustered out of the service.

I was on my way home, back to my wife and family, back to the life of the "home guard." Or so I believed at the time.

CHAPTER 12

THE IRON ROAD KEPT CALLING MY HEART

Following my return to civilian life in 1945 I quickly went back to work as a cement mason, my affection for the hobos and the hobo life notwithstanding.

Alice and Karen were in school at this time which made it impractical for Wanda and the girls to accompany me when I took an out-of-town job. But, when I was home I saw to it that I spent every free moment with my family. I carried my own love for the outdoors into my family life; we took frequent camping trips and I taught the girls much of what I had learned about living in the field. They came to find as much pleasure in this recreational activity as I did and have continued this pleasurable pursuit in their own adult lives.

I also retained my interest in amateur wrestling, entering and winning many championships in the 155-pound class, including a seven-state regional title while working in Maryland. While on a job in Arkansas, I accepted the challenge of a group of Japanese wrestlers who were in the U.S. on an amateur wrestling tour. I found them to be excellent wrestlers but managed to win the bouts I had with their best team members in my weight class. It was not unusual for me to come home after a hard day's work, shower, eat dinner and head for the nearest YMCA to work out or to participate in a match.

However, the years were catching up to me—the years and intemperate living—and finally, at age thirty-five, I had to give up my favorite sport.

The "intemperate living" was a growing tendency to spend too much time in bars with fellow cement masons. Over a period of about fifteen years my drinking grew into a serious habit and caused me a great deal of heartache. This sad failing resulted in the only time that Wanda seriously considered breaking up, once telling me that if I couldn't control my growing alcohol dependency then I should pack my clothes and move out.

Over the years I developed a great feeling of pride in my abilities as a cement mason and in the work I produced. Eventually, I took to marking my efforts much as an artist would sign a canvas.

I had learned during my years on the road that the American Indian considered the maple leaf as being "good medicine," having powers of good luck. With this in mind, I began carrying a sack of maple leafs with me whenever I went on a job and when I had finished, whether it was a sidewalk or a parking lot, a bit of freeway or a bridge, I would press a leaf into the still wet concrete, leaving a permanent impression. Before long other masons became aware of this practice and were able to identify my work when they happened upon it.

Once, while working on a bridge in Ohio, my foreman observed me pressing a leaf into the cement and ordered me to remove it and smooth over the surface. When I refused he went to the job supervisor and told him that I had refused to trowel over the impression the leaf had made.

"Just leave that alone," the supervisor said. "If you take that leaf out of there this bridge is liable to fall down."

. . .

Although I had given up my hobo life when Wanda and I had married, I had never given up my love of the freedom of the open road. Each spring, when the trees sprouted and the flowers appeared, I felt an unmistakable tug, a pulling at my heart that called me back to the iron road. It was a nagging longing that I had to annually put down. I succeeded in doing so for nearly thirty years. But there were pressures weighing down on me that ultimately would drive me back to the freight yards and the hobo jungles.

The years of kneeling for long hours on damp ground and in all kinds of weather had produced a progressive deterioration in my right hip and a growing discomfort in my knees, resulting in a gnawing pain that persisted day and night. My drinking became a convenient and not ineffective means to ease the discomfort I was experiencing.

By 1968, my daughters were grown and out on their own. Wanda had become a physiotherapist and was earning a comfortable income. The necessity of maintaining a traditional husband/father role was no longer relevant. The call of the iron road could, if I chose, be answered once more. I decided that I would satisfy my yearning to ride the rails by taking short trips, primarily on weekends.

There were at that time a number of railroad restoration groups and societies springing up around the country encouraged by people who remembered, as I did, the thrill of riding trains pulled by steam engines and who wanted to experience that thrill again.

I was immediately attracted to this movement and began seeking out the excursions that were organized and operated by these select groups. I would journey to where the pleasure runs were taking place and offer to buy a ticket to ride on the trains. I adopted the hobo style of dress; an old and baggy dark suit that frequently had a hole or two, a battered floppy hat and walking boots that had no laces but were held on my feet by large rubber bands. And, because of my hip problem, I began carrying a long staff or walking stick fashioned from a section of tree limb that had attracted my eye and which I'd smoothed and polished to a fine luster. I also grew a beard and moustache, the ends of which I waxed and twisted into sharp points.

Apparently my appearance, which didn't seem to bother those who flocked to ride the trains, became a source of discomfort to those who had organized the trips. I began encountering difficulty in obtaining tickets to the excursions, receiving, instead, excuses that the rides had been sold out or that the trips were restricted to those who belonged to the sponsoring society. I went so far as to obtain membership in several such organizations in an attempt to head off this snobbish elitism. But it didn't make matters much better. Hobos were considered too low class to ride inside their trains.

Finally, I decided that if I couldn't ride as a paying passenger, I would ride as a hobo. I began going to the starting point for the trip and, after finding a place somewhere in the yards or at the depot where I felt I could board the train safely, I would catch the hand holds on the outside of the passenger cars and swing myself up to the space between the coal tender and the baggage car, positioning myself in the covered space that serves as a connecting walkway between two passenger cars. The flexible material designed to protect passengers from the elements when moving between cars is called "the blind," and a hobo in this space is said to be "blind baggage." Clinging to the sides between two passenger cars on the outside of the flexible covers was called "riding the blind."

On one such ride from Haggerstown, Maryland, to Baltimore the train stopped partway to allow the passengers who wanted to take photographs to get off. The train then backed up for about a mile and made a speed pass for a photo or recording opportunity. When the 700 to 800 passengers reboarded, I climbed inside one of the coaches with them. The conductor heard that a hobo was on board and began looking for me. Just before he got to the car I was on, the passengers, having heard what was happening, encouraged me to conceal myself.

"Here, hide under this seat," or "Hide under my coat," or "Get in the rest room and I'll block the door."

The excursion was scheduled as an overnighter, staying in Baltimore and returning to Haggerstown the following day.

The next morning I presented myself at the depot, preparing to board the train for the trip back. But I was stopped by a group of volunteer guards and local police the railroad society had recruited for the purpose of keeping "that dirty bum" from riding the train back. They refused to allow me near the train.

"Look," I told the head guard, "You go back to that fancy parlor car that's reserved for the society officers and you tell them I'm a paid-up member of this society, I'm prepared to pay for the ticket and if he refuses, I'll sue the whole damned bunch of you. I left my car in Haggerstown and I'm riding this train back to get it. Now, you tell him that."

They held up the train while the guard conferred with the society members and the passengers shouted, "Let him ride, let the old hobo ride." Pretty soon the guard returned and instructed the conductor that I was to be permitted to ride the train but that he was to collect the twenty-five-dollar round-trip fare from me. After the train started the conductor came around and demanded the money. I paid him—in nickels and dimes I'd brought with me in a coffee can—much to the delight of the passengers.

The following year I heard that there was to be a special

run from Elizabeth, New Jersey, to Philadelphia. It would be a wonderful ride, I thought, and immediately sent for two tickets—for Wanda and me—but the sponsoring group, who had become familiar with me and my habit of showing up in ragged clothes, floppy shoes and a bedroll, said, in effect, "You're not going to ride our train."

Their attitude really teed me off, so I wrote back and informed them, "I'm willing to pay for the ride, but if you won't let me buy a ticket, I'll ride your train anyhow."

Wanda, who by this time was supportive of my weekend train-riding "hobby," drove me to New Jersey. The train was scheduled to leave at eight in the morning. We arrived about six so I would have time to scout the area and determine where the best spot to board the train would be. I cased the place like a bank robber and when the train pulled in about seven a.m. I had discovered that there was a cement culvert just ahead of where it was stopped at the depot that offered a perfect place for me to hide while awaiting the train to pass by. It had a cement abutment that rose about four feet above the roadbed which, if I stood on it, would put me at a convenient level to grab the handholds on the outside of the blind as the train came by.

At the depot I could see about thirty security guards, brought in by the run's sponsors to make certain that I didn't fulfill my threat. They were standing on the top of the train, on the coal tender, at the boarding gates and on the roof of the depot. They were just as determined to keep me off that train as I was determined to ride it.

It was cold that morning, standing down in the culvert with the sun not high enough to warm me. I had brought a bottle of cheap red wine with me and while I waited I drank the wine. By the time the train began to move I was quite warm and very confident about getting on board.

As the train started to pull out, I peeked out of the culvert and noticed that the guards had all gone inside, presuming that I'd abandoned my plan to ride the train.

As the locomotive came by, steadily picking up speed, its whistle blowing loudly, I jumped out of the culvert, ran up onto the abutment and reached for the handhold of the first car. I missed it, barely keeping my balance. When I reached for the next one the train had accelerated to probably thirty or thirty-five miles an hour. Grabbing the handholds of the speeding train jerked me off the abutment and damn near pulled my arms out of their sockets. If it hadn't been for my years working in concrete, which had toughened and strengthened my arms and shoulders, I probably would have fallen and been pulled beneath the wheels.

The tour was advertised as a speed run with one stop in Plainfield, New Jersey. I had told Wanda to meet me there; the short run from Elizabeth would be sufficient to prove that I could ride their train as I'd promised. However, it was somewhat more than I'd bargained for; one foot on a small ledge on each of the connecting cars, hanging on with both hands to the outside of a train moving down the tracks at eighty miles an hour was not just exciting, it was downright terrifying, especially when we met a train traveling at high speed in the opposite direction. The turbulence created nearly pulled me from my tiny perch. It was like being in the middle of a tornado.

There was considerable interest in the old trains and hundreds of people lined the tracks along the route to watch the old steam locomotive and restored passenger cars flash by. I've often wondered how much added fascination they received when they noticed a ragged hobo hanging on for dear life, occasionally waving as the train went by. There were a great many who were taking pictures that day who probably were too busy focusing their cameras for a clear shot and didn't notice me at that time. I can only imagine their amazement when their photos came back from the processor and they saw this old dude plastered on the outside of the railroad car. No doubt many have preserved these unusual shots, but to my knowledge neither the railroad society, nor the newspapers ever acknowledged my unauthorized presence on that much publicized run.

As we neared Plainfield a passenger—probably a retired locomotive engineer or fireman—stuck his head out the passenger car window just ahead of where I was located. He had his cap turned backwards and was wearing goggles, just eating up the smoke and having a wonderful time.

I yelled to attract his attention and when he turned and saw me I shouted: "How do you like your ride?"

He did a couple of quick takes and then pulled his head back inside. Almost immediately windows started going up all along that side of the train and people were sticking their heads out to see this incredible sight. The guards were leaning out, too, and gesturing at me, obviously furious. I waved to them all.

Soon the coach door next to where I was hanging on opened and a guard shouted: "We're stopping in Plainfield and you're getting off; you're not gonna stay on this train."

"That's okay. Plainfield is as far as I planned to go," I smiled and shouted back.

As soon as we pulled into the depot, they grabbed me as if I was a bank thief. I was covered with soot, black and dirty as I could be but I maintained my dignity.

"Take your hands off me," I insisted. "I'm not going to get back on your train; I just wanted to prove that I could ride on it whether you wanted me to or not." Still, they ushered me away from the depot and had the police stand guard over me until the train had pulled out.

Although I hadn't bought a ticket, the ride had cost me nonetheless. It was the wildest ride I'd ever taken, and unquestionably the most frightening; my jaw muscles had been so tensed up that I couldn't chew for days; my arms and legs throbbed with pain and I found it difficult to sleep for many days thereafter. But I've always been pleased and proud that I made that run.

I continued to ride freights and historic passenger runs on weekends through 1969. At the same time I was working for the U.S. Army, teaching classes in concrete work to army engineer students at Fort Belvoir, Virginia.

My hip was giving me more trouble all the time. I couldn't climb ladders or scaffolds any longer; I could spend only short periods kneeling and found it increasingly difficult to carry anything but the lightest objects. My years as a cement mason were obviously coming to an end. I was fifty-five and could no longer practice my trade. It was a very low point in my life.

But there was but one profession for which I was now still qualified; I could return to the life of a professional hobo. For thirty years the iron road had been calling my heart. Now I decided I would answer that call.

CHAPTER 13
ON THE ROAD AGAIN

My daughters were grown, Wanda was firmly installed in a well-paying profession and I felt that I wasn't really needed at home any longer. My hip and my knees made it impossible to work as a cement mason and I was drinking heavily—sometimes as much as two fifths of whiskey a day. A change in the direction of my life was definitely indicated.

During 1968 and 1969 I had been taking frequent trips on the freights, beginning as weekend tours, slowly building up to a week at a time. After leaving my job with the army I quickly increased my travels, extending the trips over greater distances and staying away for longer periods of time.

As I roamed about the country I discovered that a great many changes had occurred during my more than thirty-year absence. The steam locomotives had all disappeared on the regular runs, leaving a sad and irreplaceable void, which the diesel engines were never able to fill.

There had always been something strange and wonderful about these huge, hulking machines that moaned and groaned and belched black, sooty smoke and hot cinders and ash. They were dirty and ungainly and totally lacking in any artistic grace. Yet, even in their noisy puffing and wheezing, there was a majesty, an elegance that the diesels have never been able to match. Each steam locomotive had its own personality, its own charm that set it apart from all others; the experienced railroaders—whether train crews or frequent riders—were able to recognize individual locomotives by their look or their sound.

Even the men who operated them gave the steam locomotives a familiar and easily recognizable personality. Many engineers had their own whistles which they brought with them to their assigned engine, whistles that, in their construction, gave them unique sounds and which were identifiable from the manner in which they were played. Perhaps the most famous railroad engineer of all time was the legendary Casey Jones who, on a dark night in Mississippi, crashed his speeding train into the rear of a parked freight. Casey had a specially constructed five-fluted whistle that he insisted be installed on every locomotive he drove.

The low, mournful moan of the steam locomotives' whistles had thrilled and excited many a youth late at night as they echoed through the valleys and over the flatlands of America. Nor has that thrill been forgotten by adults. Today, when a restored steam engine rumbles down the tracks at railroad festivals, countless tape recorders are switched on to capture and preserve that wonderful sound.

In 1969, when I began to seriously ride the trains again, I discovered that with the passing of the steam locomotives, the hobo himself was rapidly fading into history. Only a handful continued to ride the trains; the hobo jungles were largely abandoned. The railroads had cut back, there just weren't as many trains running the line any longer, making travel more difficult for the 'bo. The boxcar had been "modernized," made larger and more difficult to board, and the doors were kept locked to cut down on the wind resistance that ate up diesel fuel and reduced speed.

Many of the rail lines were in very bad condition, probably the worst in history. The tracks were so poorly maintained that numerous derailments were occurring and a great many people—including hobos—were being killed and injured. One hobo, on a freight that derailed, was trapped in the wreckage for three days before being found and released. It was the last time he would ride the trains.

Passenger runs were rapidly being phased out of service. In 1969, I rode the last run of the Erie and Lackawana's Lake City Limited, which made daily trips between New York City and Chicago. It was ten degrees above zero and snowing very hard as I climbed on the small vestibule at the end of the last car. I rode from Lima, Ohio, to Anderson, Indiana. When the train pulled into Anderson, I was standing in about three feet of snow that had been blown into the open space and was nearly frozen to death. But I made at least part of that last run. Because it appeared that passenger rail service was to become extinct in the United States, I made as many of these "final runs" as possible. Later, of course, Amtrak would revive this form of transportation and, if not restore it to its once thriving condition, would preserve some of the pleasures that were once found in this wonderfully relaxing form of travel.

When I returned to hoboing I discovered that even the bulls were different; there weren't as many of them anymore and those that remained tended to largely ignore the hobos riding their freights. "We just don't have the manpower to arrest them or throw them off the trains," the head of one railroad's security police was quoted as saying. "As long as they don't cause no trouble we leave them alone." The train crews had become more understanding and helpful, too. When I went into a yard I could go to the brakeman's shack and ask what trains were leaving and where they were headed and they would always tell me and point out the trains ready to leave.

The transients were gone, as were the transit bureaus. Winos and bums could still be found in the cities and towns, but few were riding the trains.

The life on the road to which I returned in 1970 was far different than the one I had left in the 1930s. And yet the magic of the road was still there and the lure I felt was just as strong as it had ever been.

Because the hobo jungles had disappeared, the few hobos that remained had to reconstruct them. The winos had taken over the few areas near the towns that were left, which meant that we had to go farther from the city limits, move a greater distance down the rivers to set up a place to have a campfire and a decent place to spread a bedroll. We discovered that junk yards, which could be found around most every city or town, offered great possibilities for the hobo; there was always material available for our use, such as car seats which we could place around the fires. Other spots we sought out were underpasses and bridges which provided shelter from the rain.

Contrary to the image many people have of today's skeptical and suspicious society, the hobo in the 1970s could still find work in exchange for a meal or a little food. Housewives remained an excellent resource for food in exchange for a few chores; there were bushes to trim, windows to wash, lawns to be cut and housewives who were glad to have a hobo show up to tend to the small jobs that husbands and children so diligently avoided—that is, the older housewives were. The younger women tended to be frightened of bearded old men in tattered clothes knocking on their back doors. It became a rule of thumb for 'bos to look for housewives over the age of thirty-five. They always had several items of canned goods that they had bought and never used and were delighted to hand out to a hobo who was willing to do a little work.

Supermarkets were another excellent place to earn a bit of meat or fresh fruit or vegetables. There are always odd jobs to be done at the back of the markets—vegetables to be washed or bagged, storage areas to be cleaned, boxes to be flattened and bundled and carried out. In a short time a hobo could learn what jobs needed to be done, approach the store manager and suggest that he tend to the chores in exchange for a bit of food.

My trips away from Wanda became more frequent and lasted longer each time. Although I never told her, she always knew when I was getting ready to leave.

"We did the grocery shopping together, and Maurice always bought a lot of cookies, cakes and chips; the things men like," she explains when asked about our life together. "When he was planning to go on one of his trips he wouldn't buy any of those things and I knew he would be leaving. I'd get home from work and there would be a note saying good-bye."

From a short few days I graduated to a week or more, then to as much as six months of hoboing. I found some of the old-time hobos I'd met when on the road in the 1930s, men like Slow-Motion Shorty and Fry Pan Jack and I began traveling with them, going nowhere but always going, catching any freight that was heading out.

It was exciting to be free again, to have no schedule to keep, to be unrestricted and responsible to no one but ourselves and to that time and place. The air was fresher and cleaner, the sun was warmer and brighter, the campfires were more comforting and colorful.

We traveled over much of the country, riding freights where we could, occasionally hitchhiking when there were no trains to catch, always meeting new people who would become "friends for life," people who would take the time to eagerly listen as we told them of our adventures and the glories of the open road.

It was about this time that I acquired my road name, Steam Train.

I had always called myself Idaho, the nickname my school friends and the old hobos had called me. But when I started traveling around looking for the passenger runs of the restored steam locomotives, the press began anticipating that I would show up to ride the old trains. "That steam train guy will probably be here," they would say. Finally, Hank Harvey of the Toledo *Blade*, who had become acquainted with me and my travels, started referring to me in his columns as "Steam Train Maury." The name stuck; I liked it and adopted it as my own.

Going back on the road enabled me to hone and refine my cooking skills, particularly in the making of the famous hobo stew. There is, I've found, some misunderstanding on the part of the general public about hobo stew. Many seem to believe that this concoction is made from whatever scraps of food can be found, with no concern for the ingredients, their quantity or preparation. This isn't true. While there is no specific recipe for the ingredients of hobo stew, there are traditional methods employed in the making of this flavorful dish.

I've also found some confusion between so-called "Mulligan stew" and that which the hobo has made for a century or more. A few years ago a reporter made the incorrect statement that "Mulligan was like Kilroy—no one ever saw him; he was a fictitious character."

Although his first name has been lost to history, there was, indeed, a cook named Mulligan. One of the many Irishmen who came to this country to work as "gandy dancers," or section hands helping build the transcontinental railroads, Mulligan became a "gang cook" for the construction crews working west. Mulligan became famous for his excellent stew, which consisted of huge chunks of meat—buffalo, when it was available, beef at other times—large pieces of potatoes and carrots and other vegetables, when they could be obtained, and various herbs which could be found along the route. The major difference between Mulligan stew and beef or meat stews made at home was the use of corn meal as a thickening agent rather than the flour or corn starch usually added by a housewife. Corn meal was used because it served both as a thickener and as an expander, when necessary, to feed a greater number of diners. Corn meal is a very nutritious food in itself. Added to stew it gave it a pleasant yellow color and a smooth, pleasing flavor.

Hobo stew employs the same ingredients as Mulligan stew—with one important exception—but differs in the size of the cuts of meat and vegetables used in the recipe. Hobos fine-cut their pieces of meat and vegetables. This was originally done for two basic reasons. First of all, when a "crumb boss"—a hobo cook—made a batch of stew for a small number of men, it was more difficult to give an equal amount of meat and vegetables to each man if the chunks were large; some would get several pieces of meat while others might have no meat at all; some would be served mostly vegetables while others would have all meat. The small, bite-sized pieces were easily mixed together and served up with equal amounts of all ingredients. The second reason for fine-cutting the ingredients was to speed up the cooking time. In the hobo jungles, 'bos were coming and going at all times, some having to "catch out" earlier than others, requiring the common meal be made quickly to insure that everyone who had contributed to the meal had the opportunity of being fed before they had to leave.

The one elment found in hobo stew and in no other is a legacy from the American Indians, who believed that the many minerals found in granite stones could be boiled out and consumed to give added strength in times of famine or harsh winters. The hobos began using the stones in their stew; the crumb bosses carried a number of them in their bindles. Often they would bury a small cache of the granite in the bushes or beneath a marker near their jungles for other cooks arriving later. The stones had another, more pragmatic purpose in making hobo stew; the stones roll around the bottom of the pot when the cook stirs the stew, preventing the ingredients from sticking and burning, thereby spoiling the batch.

While the exact recipe for "authentic" hobo stew varies from one crumb boss to another, these are the instructions for making basic, genuine hobo stew for fifty people.

HOBO STEW

Render all fat out of 6 to 8 lbs bite-sized cut beef or hamburger.
Combine in large iron pot:

6 lbs potatoes
6 lbs carrots
2–3 lbs onions
2 bunches celery
1 or 2 heads cabbage
1 gal whole kernel corn
1 gal tomato juice (2 gals is better)
2 family-sized bottles soy sauce
1 bottle Louisiana Hot Sauce (to taste)
2 tablespoons pure garlic powder
1 tablespoon Italian herbs
3 or 4 bay leaves
1 lb margarine
pure corn meal to desired thickness

To a large iron pot add cooked meat (after fat has been rendered off) and all other ingredients except margarine and corn meal with sufficient water to cover contents with about two inches of water. Bring to a slow boil and cook for about two hours.
Add margarine and then corn meal (be certain you use pure corn meal with no additives.)
Boil for an additional half hour, stirring almost constantly.

Serve in large plates or bowls.
Do not add salt. Permit individuals to salt to their own taste.

Of course, this recipe can be modified to accommodate a smaller batch of this delicious stew.

. . .

I would return to Toledo from my journeys for a while and then the call of the iron road would beckon again. I'd pack my bedroll, don my old hobo clothes, grab my battered hat and my walking stick and I'd be off again, searching for another adventure, another town, another "friend for life."

When I took a trip I would always find time to call home occasionally—collect—to let Wanda know where I was and that I was all right.

In 1971 I left on an indefinite, and—as usual—unannounced trip. Unfortunately, I picked the wrong time to telephone home. It was about nine in the evening of the day I'd left and Wanda had just fallen asleep after having come home from a very hard and exhausting day at the hospital. She had found my note, fixed herself some eggs, taken a bath and collapsed into bed. Then the phone rang, jolting her out of a deep sleep. She picked it up and heard the operator announce that there was a collect call from Maurice Graham.

"Will you accept the charges?" the operator asked.

"No, I won't!" Wanda responded, slamming the receiver down on the startled telephone operator and a stunned Maurice Graham.

I assumed that she was disgusted with me and my wandering ways. It would be eight years before I would call her again, and almost ten before I'd return home to stay.

I would, however, call my daughters periodically to find out how Wanda was and to let her know how I was. On our thirty-eighth wedding anniversary I sent her a dozen yellow roses—her favorite flower. I had a card included which said, simply: "I remembered the day and happy anniversary."

She was able to maintain some knowledge of my whereabouts and what I was doing. In 1973 I was elected King of the Hobos for the first time; there was the usual newspaper publicity, and she saw a television news item about the hobo convention. A friend—one of the few who knew Wanda and I were married—asked her if she didn't feel jealous over the attention I was getting and the adventures I was experiencing. She replied: "No. I say, more power to him, if that's what he wants."

Those friends who were aware of our unusual marriage would urge Wanda to "get rid of him." But she would shake her head and insist that I was her husband and she couldn't consider such a move.

Throughout the time I was gone she took care of the house or apartment, did the small chores that a man would normally do—cutting the grass in the summer and shoveling the snow in the winter. Her neighbors assumed she was a widow or divorced; she never talked about her husband, never told them she had married a hobo whose itchy feet kept him constantly on the road.

I began making visits to Toledo starting in 1978. I called Wanda one evening and she accepted my call. I told her, "I'm out at the rail yards. I'd like to take you to dinner but you know I don't have any money." I didn't have a car, either. She came and picked me up. We went to dinner and she picked up the check. Then she drove me back to the rail yards.

She thought this role reversal was funny then and still laughs about it today.

CHAPTER 14

AND SUDDENLY THEY LOVE US

By the time I was back on the road, traveling full time, the attitude of much of the public about the hobo had changed. There was a better understanding of who the hobo was and a clearer distinction between him and the other people on the road.

Although many continue to this day to use the terms hobo, tramp and bum interchangeably, the hobo has captured a warm spot in the public heart that was not widespread when I went on the road as a teenager.

The hobo is looked on today as a colorful old gent, kindly and soft-spoken, a harmless recluse quietly going about his life never harming anyone. The hobo was always that way, but it took a hundred years for the public to find that out.

While, during the 1970s, there were still instances

when railroad police continued to harass the 'bos, it was not nearly as prevalent as it once had been. Local police occasionally ran men of the road out of town, but generally they were understanding and, as much as they were able, helpful to the traveler.

Because the railroads were dying, it was necessary to hitchhike much more than I had in earlier years. But I soon discovered that this method of travel offered a tremendous opportunity to meet and make wonderful friends for life.

A number of times I was picked up by a motorist and, after several miles of telling him stories of my experiences on the road, I would be invited to go home with him for dinner and sometimes a night's rest.

This impulsive hospitality occasionally caused some minor difficulty. The generous man would have to face the silent wrath of his wife who was suddenly confronted not just with an unexpected dinner guest, but with a ragged old "bum" who had also been asked to stay the night.

I later discovered that some of these silently suffering women were convinced that they would be butchered in their beds that night, although they had homicidal thoughts of their own directed to their thoughtless spouse who had brought me into their homes.

Yet, in spite of the rude introduction they had experienced, these women took me into their hearts and I became a close and welcome member of their families. I continue corresponding with many of these couples and visit with them whenever I'm in their area. In one case, an Indiana couple I had come to know well later divorced and went their separate ways, one moving to Georgia, the other to Illinois, but both maintained a regular correspondence with me and made me welcome when I traveled their way. I got to know whole families, and still hear from and visit with the now-grown children.

I was once picked up by a professor of music at Iowa State University. We traveled together for more than a hundred miles, during which time we became good friends. He had told me that he traveled around the state entertaining schoolchildren and other gatherings with a wide selection of folk songs he had learned. Later I received a letter from him informing me that as the result of the time we'd spent together on that ride he had composed a song about "this old hobo and some of the adventures that he'd lived while on the road." He said it had fast become one of the best-loved songs he performed and was frequently requested. I've had five songs written about me over the years, some by very accomplished musicians, but I think that one was the first and probably the most flattering.

Hitching a ride wasn't always met with enthusiastic success. When I first returned to the road, one of my favorite trips was across Michigan to Ludington, on the eastern shore of Lake Michigan. There, the Chesapeake and Ohio Railroad ran an auto-train ferry across the lake to Wisconsin. The ferry was popular among tourists because of the pleasant three-and-a-half to four-hour boat ride; the trains, trucks and buses using the service found it a practical and time-saving means of getting from Michigan to Wisconsin. For me it was an enjoyable way to bypass the hectic crush of Chicago.

The ferry carried twelve freight cars—which were loaded before any other vehicles—with the balance made up of cars, trucks and buses. To ride the ferry on one of the railroad cars it was necessary to get into the yard and determine which cars parked there would be among the dozen to be put aboard. Then it required finding a suitable spot on one of the cars, which was not always an easy task. If it proved impossible to ride across the lake using one of the freight cars, I would move back to the road leading to the docks and attempt to hitch a ride in one of the autos. On one occasion I asked for and received permission to cross aboard a bus that carried a football team headed to Wisconsin for a game.

The major problem in getting across the lake on the

ferry was the captain commanding the boat. He had observed me in the yard several times and had heard that members of the boat crew were bringing coffee and sandwiches to me while they worked to tie down or chock the vehicles below decks. Under company regulations, once the ferry had been loaded, the passengers were required to move to the upper decks where there were places to get something to eat and deck chairs and benches both inside, when the weather was cold or wet, and out on deck, when conditions were favorable. Only the crew was permitted to remain below decks.

The captain was furious at me for several reasons. To begin with, he objected to someone with my tattered appearance being aboard his boat; he objected even more to the fact that I was a nonpaying passenger; he objected to his crew feeding and caring for my comforts instead of strictly obeying his orders; and finally he objected to my always being able to get aboard and make the trip in spite of his insistence that I not be allowed on his vessel.

A few years ago, I met a retired officer who had served aboard the ferry. The man told me how the captain would spot me near his boat and would shout to the other officers:

"Watch that old guy. Do not let him get near this ship."

Later, when we had docked in Wisconsin, he would be on the bridge watching the unloading when he'd again spot me in the yard. He would become enraged.

"I told you men to watch him, to keep him off this ship."

"We did watch him," the officers would respond.

"Then how the hell did he get over here?"

The retired officer told me how it had become a source of amusement among the men that I was always able to frustrate the captain's attempt to keep me from making the lake crossing. It became a joke and a game with them, but it may have taken years off that unfortunate captain's life.

There were many people who showed kindness and hospitality in other ways. Once in Peru, Illinois, I found myself without a place to sleep, with a severe thunderstorm approaching. Spotting a car dealership, I began checking the autos on the used car lot to see if any were unlocked. Fortunately, an old van parked near the back of the lot was open, and I crawled inside and spent a comfortable, dry night.

The next morning I was awake early and walked to a nearby restaurant for some breakfast. When I had finished I noticed that the dealership was open for business, so I returned and asked to speak to the manager. The man who owned the Buick dealership came out and I explained what I had done the previous night, telling him: "You should always have an old car parked at the back of your lot that's unlocked for people on the road to get in out of the weather. Actually, you'll find it's not just an act of kindness, but it can save damage to your newer cars by someone who's desperate enough to break a window or door to get in if all the doors are locked."

"That's a good idea," he said, and promised to have just such a vehicle there.

I wrote to him for many years thereafter and we became good friends.

One hitched ride proved to be particularly terrifying for the driver. I was passing through Chicago in the early 1970s on my way west. As the train was pulling into the south Chicago yards, I decided I would take up a friend on his offer to come and pick me up any time I was in town. He lived in Chicago and it seemed like a good opportunity to visit with him for a while. The problem was that it was about two in the morning when I got in and I was having trouble finding a place open where I could use the telephone. That part of Chicago has always been an extremely tough part of town. As a matter of fact, I suspect it's a very tough part of the world. There was no one on the streets, no bars or restaurants were open in that area and it was incredibly dark in the section bordering the rail yards.

I wandered around for a while without finding any sign of life. Then I noticed a light in a dingy looking building across the street from the yards. I walked up and knocked on the door. Soon a huge, menacing black man appeared. He looked at me as though he couldn't believe what he was seeing. I assumed it was my hobo clothing that surprised him. After a long moment he asked what I wanted. I explained that I had just gotten off a freight and wanted to call a friend to come down and pick me up. He still looked incredulous, but he swung the door open and motioned for me to come in.

I realized immediately that I had stumbled into an after-hours drinking place—a "blind pig." The men in the room, all black and tough-looking, who had been laughing and talking loudly when I came through the door, suddenly grew deathly still; each had turned in my direction and was studying me carefully. It wasn't too difficult to feel genuine hostility in the room and I felt very threatened and began to wonder if I'd be able to get out of there with my skin intact.

"Don't you know, white man, that it ain't safe for you to be walkin' 'round down in this part of town?" one of the men asked.

"Well," I explained, "I just got off a train and I was trying to find a telephone to call a friend to come pick me up."

"What'd'ya mean, you just got off a train?" another wanted to know.

I told them I was a hobo and that I had come into the yards on a freight.

"You mean an old dude like you rides freight trains?"

I allowed as how I did.

"How'd you get out 'a them yards, they got a fence forty feet high?"

The fence was tall, too tall for me to crawl over, but I had found a gap near a drainage culvert and had dug out enough of the dirt and gravel to squeeze my way under.

"They got cops all over the place. How'd you get by them?"

"I just stayed down low to the ground until they'd passed," I told them.

"Well I'll be," the bulky bartender said, bursting into laughter that was echoed by the rest in the large room. "This old dude's a real hobo all right."

After that I was accepted by everyone there. They showed me to the phone and let me call my friend.

When he came on the phone I told him that, while I knew it was late, I was taking him up on his invitation and would he please come and pick me up.

"Where are you?" he asked sleepily.

I gave him my location.

"WHAT? Are you CRAZY? You'll get yourself killed down there, you old fool."

I told him I was quite safe, that I was in a black blind pig.

"You expect ME to come down THERE at this time of night? You ARE crazy."

He insisted that he wouldn't dream of going into that neighborhood at two in the morning, that he was reluctant to venture there in broad daylight.

However, after some discussion he agreed that he would take his life into his hands and come to get me, on the condition that he would not get out of his car, that he would honk his horn when he drove up to the front of the drinking place and that I had better be there waiting because he was not going to hang around.

While I waited, I entertained the men in the bar with some tales of my experiences running from railroad bulls and other exciting stories of my life on the road. They were obviously charmed, bought me drinks and sat listening intently to everything I said, laughing loudly at my stories.

The time sped by and I was thoroughly enjoying myself when we heard a car horn outside.

"That must be your friend," the bartender said, and everyone moaned in disappointment.

I thanked them for the drinks and the hospitality, and they all assured me that any time I was in the area I was welcome to stop back and see them.

"You'll be safe down here," the bartender said, shaking my hand.

We all moved outside, which gave my friend a frightening moment as his car was surrounded. But he unlocked the passenger door and let me in. One of the men bent down at the driver's window and pointed a finger at my friend.

"You take good care of this old dude, y' hear?"

My friend nodded nervously and sped off.

"The next time you come into town, don't you dare call me from down here. I don't care what time it is."

We had a pleasant visit and I left town the next day. But since then I've not been able to get in touch with him, he's never answered my letters and his phone number has been changed.

I found bars to be among the most hospitable places during the years I was drinking heavily. I never once mooched a drink, never panhandled for booze. If I didn't have money to buy a drink I didn't go into bars. But I did discover that I didn't have to buy. I would wander into a tavern, order a drink and start talking to the patrons around me. It was always easy to engage people in conversation; my unusual manner of dress, the bedroll I carried and my strange walking stick—or staff—always elicited questions.

Once I explained that I was a hobo, I had a guaranteed audience and would not have to buy a drink the rest of the night. The bartenders made certain I always had a full glass in front of me; I was great for business. The customers loved it and would hang around—buying drinks—as long as they could stand up. And when they left there was always another group to replace them. I often drank four different crowds under the table in a single evening. I've been in the basement bar of the Waldorf Astoria Hotel in New York, an exclusive watering hole populated by the Wall Street crowd, and outdone the stock brokers who, I quickly discovered, are a two-fisted drinking bunch.

Like the other places I was visiting in those days, I found that the people of the 1970s appreciated the hobo. After generations of being looked down upon by most of society, suddenly they loved us.

The housewives continued to hand out food in exchange for chores but there seemed—in the 1970s at least—to be more of them, and the quantity of food they were willing to provide seemed to have increased.

Once, while riding the freights through Nebraska, I had gone a couple of days without food. This would happen at times, when I was in a hurry to get somewhere or when there were fewer trains available, and I hated to leave a train for fear that I might not be able to catch another for several days.

After two days without a decent meal, I was desperate. About supper time one evening, the train I was riding stopped in a small Nebraska town and I learned from one of the train crew that it would be there for an hour or so, time enough for me to call at a few houses and ask to trade some chores for food. I wanted to get something I could carry back to the train and eat when the freight resumed its journey.

The woman at the first house I called at said that she had no work for me to do, but that they had just finished eating and there were leftovers that I was welcome to. She told me the food was still hot and told me to come in and help myself. Sometimes a housewife would bring a plate of food to the back porch and allow you to sit there and eat.

As was the traditional hobo practice, I asked if she could place something in a paper bag and hand it out to me.

"No, there's mashed potatoes and gravy, canned corn and beef," she replied. "There's plenty here and it's hot. Now you just come in and sit down at the table."

I was starving and it smelled so good, I went in. The woman kept piling my plate and ordering me to eat.

She insisted I eat a full meal right there. But when she looked away I stuffed a few biscuits in my pocket to take with me.

When I had finished I thanked her sincerely and left. I still wanted to get some food I could take with me so I went to a house a few doors away. The second woman pulled the same thing on me, insisting that I come in for a sit-down meal.

I begged her to just hand me out something, but she wouldn't hear of it. Again I had to sit at the table and consume a hearty meal of meat and potatoes and gravy and bread and biscuits and vegetables. She stood over me, urging me to have another helping. Again I managed to secrete a few biscuits and a slice or two of bread in my pockets. I even tried rolling a bit of mashed potatoes and gravy in a piece of bread.

Once outside, I transferred what I had into a paper bag I always carried with me. I was absolutely *stuffed* but I still did not have enough in the bag to make much difference if I wasn't able to get off the train again soon.

I thought I would have enough time before the train was scheduled to leave to make one more attempt at a handout.

The third house I called on proved the same as the first two. The family was still seated at the table and when I asked the man of the house if I could work for a small bag of food, he all but dragged me into the house.

"We won't let no hungry man go away without eating," he said as he propelled me toward the table heaped with a full dinner menu. "We got food here to throw away. You come on in here and eat."

"Could you please put something in a sack? I've got to catch a train," I pleaded.

"Can't put it in a sack," the woman said. "Sit down. It won't take long, you can gulp it down in just a few minutes."

There were many times in past years when all they could give me was a few slices of bread which could, when I was very hungry, taste as good as a steak. I'd eat them (the slices) in small pieces and I can remember how delicious it was when I had gone without several meals. Now, I couldn't escape with just a crust.

When I had finally convinced the family that I couldn't stay any longer, I headed back for the rail yards having eaten three banquets in an hour's time. My stomach was so stretched I thought it would burst and it hurt so bad I could hardly walk.

Once I had managed to drag my loaded body onto the train, I just lay in a corner and moaned. The bouncing boxcar made it that much worse. I had taken some pretty good beatings that didn't hurt as much as all that overeating had.

There were times when getting food wasn't all that easy. One old 'bo took painful precautions to overcome this problem. The Pennsylvania Kid had a constant, unreasoning terror of being caught with nothing to eat. To guard against such an eventuality, if a housewife gave him two canning jars of green beans, for example, he would save one of the jars. When he had accumulated six or seven such containers, he would find a spot near a hobo jungle and bury his store. The Kid had stocks of canned goods buried all over the country. I was with him several times when we'd come into a town and not be able to hustle enough food for a good meal. The Kid would lead me to the closest jungle and, while I was getting a fire going, he would start rummaging through a pile of rocks or old timbers, dragging things out of the way until pretty soon he'd come up with several cans of food. I've often wondered how many stashes he forgot about, how many are still out there somewhere.

Many hobos did the same thing with money. Some

would work a construction job for a while and end up with more cash than they wanted to carry on the road with them. Some, like the Pennsylvania Kid, would bury it, only to forget just where. Others would open bank accounts, leaving the money and carrying passbooks instead. Some had a dozen or more such accounts all over the country. And some would lose their passbooks and not be able to remember which banks the money was in. Some would die or get themselves killed. A fortune was scattered all over by forgetful, careless or dead hobos.

In 1972, I teamed up with Fry Pan Jack in Mason City, Iowa, for a summer of hoboing. At one point, when we hadn't had much luck with "backdoor bumming," one of us suggested that perhaps we could get some of the food stamps we'd read were being distributed to those in need.

"Why not," the other said. "After all, we're veterans, ain't we?"

We found the food stamp office and got in a line of about twenty people waiting to apply.

We felt very encouraged; everyone ahead of us was being issued books of the stamps. Surely, we whispered between ourselves, we'd get a few books, too. After all we *were* veterans.

When we got to the front of the line we were dismissed after failing to answer one simple question—what's your address?

"You can't get stamps without a permanent mailing address," we were told by an annoyed, indignant clerk as she waved us aside. Being a veteran cut no ice with her. We found later that there apparently was a way we could have become eligible for the stamps, but it would have required several weeks of processing paperwork.

We could have lied, I suppose, made up an address. But we weren't like that. We believed it was better to be truthful . . . even though hungry!

CHAPTER 15

I WOULD BE KING

There are two major hobo groups in the country, both over eighty years old.

The first was the National Hobo Convention—also known as the Tourist Union 63—founded in 1900. At least that's when they had their first convention. The gatherings themselves were not a continuing event in the early years. There were meetings of directors and other officers but it was not until 1933 that annual conventions began to be held in Britt, Iowa, and even then there was an interruption during the World War II years. The other was first called Hobos of America, Inc. and later known as Knights of the Road, Air & Seven Seas. This group is also called the American Convention and was founded by Jeff Davis in 1908.

Davis was born in Cincinnati, Ohio, in 1883. He ran

away from home when he was twelve and went to New York City where he sold newspapers for a time. Later he began wandering the country and, at various times, worked as a field harvest hand in the plains and as a mule skinner in Arizona.

He proclaimed himself King of the Hobos when he organized the American Convention, and retained absolute control until 1965, when poor health forced him to step down. During the later years of his "reign" he improved on his title, appointing himself Emperor of the Knights of the Road.

Davis fought off many attempts to wrest away control of the organization and survived several challenges to his accounting of the funds collected by the convention.

What can't be disputed, however, is the good Jeff did during more than fifty years as hobo king.

During the two world wars he sold millions of dollars' worth of war bonds. After both wars he devoted himself to raising money to help hospitalized veterans. Although, ostensibly, membership was to be restricted to those "who travel in search of work," Davis sold millions of memberships to the general public. All of the money went to the charities supported by his group; he took nothing for himself, never had an automobile, and died a poor man. He made many celebrities members of the American Hobo Convention. James Stewart, Red Skelton, the late cowboy star Tom Mix and silent film actress Marie Dressler were among those given honorary memberships. Davis died in 1968.

When Davis relinquished his crown in 1965, Gordon "Bud" Filer, a former railroad employee, became king, elected for a five-year term.

My only criticism of Davis—whom I knew well and considered a close friend—was that he had left the road in the 1930s, had gone on to "riding the cushions," and as a result, had largely lost contact with real hobos. Before the beginning of World War II, Davis claimed that hobos had disappeared from the American scene. This was grossly untrue; there were hundreds still traveling the iron road. Also, I felt that his attitude toward the tramp was ill-advised. He claimed that a tramp wouldn't work. I knew, from my own personal experience, that this simply wasn't so. A tramp, like a hobo, was more than willing to work for a meal. It was the bum and the wino who refused to do any labor, preferring to panhandle for their survival. Actually, there was only one minor difference between the tramp and the hobo and that was the means employed to travel around the country. The tramp walked or hitchhiked; the hobo usually rode the trains. The tramps never organized the way the hobos did; therefore, they were never well-represented and had no one to champion their causes or to defend them against unwarranted charges such as the one Davis had made.

The National Hobo Convention, unlike the American Convention, is composed of actual hobo men and women who have traveled or are still traveling the railroads of America. While the king is elected by the people who come to Britt for the annual convention, he must be or have been an authentic hobo.

Another difference between the two groups is how their conventions are conducted. While the National Convention is always held in Britt, with outdoor cooking and gatherings in the "jungle" there and with most of the hobos sleeping out at night, the American Convention—at least until recently—was held in various places and always at a fancy motel, with the members sleeping in air-conditioned rooms complete with television and room service.

I happened on one of their conventions in Pennsylvania once. I'd slept out in the woods behind the hotel and the next morning built a fire to make coffee. The smell of the hardwood fire, combined with that of boiling coffee, produced a strong aroma that was pulled into the hotel's air-conditioning and was spread throughout the building. People began inquiring as to the origin of the delightful fragrance.

"There's an old bum out in back that's cooking," a hotel employee announced.

A few of the conventioneers wandered out to see for themselves, but none invited me to join their group.

"He's probably one of those dirty old guys who still rides freight trains," one said.

I was just as happy they didn't invite me in. But I thought it was ironic that in front of the hotel, where they were paying fifty dollars a day to sit inside and play cards, was a large sign that said: "Welcome Hobos."

I attended my first National Hobo Convention in 1971. I'd heard about the Britt, Iowa, gathering and wanted to see it for myself.

To be honest, I wasn't very impressed. The hobos who were there spent most of their time in the local bars drinking beer. None of them were sleeping in the nice shrubbery along the tracks or cooking in a jungle. I saw a couple of them cooking coffee in an alley and not doing a very good job of it. The "king" that year was sleeping in an old abandoned jail house that was filthy, smelly and usually occupied by stray dogs.

"I can't believe this," I said to myself.

There were a few old-time 'bos attending, but they were staying outside of town to get away from the drunks.

What did impress me were the crowds that flocked to this little town: people who were genuinely interested in hobos, who wanted to learn more about them, wanted to be around them. The Britt Chamber of Commerce did a magnificent job of hosting what they called "Hobo Days." Of course they should have; except for a few years during the war, the convention had been held there every year since 1932. They had a fine parade and a number of arts and crafts booths and some rides for the children. Anywhere from five to twenty thousand people attended the convention each year. Hobos came from all over the country to be there.

But I felt that it could be greatly improved, that the hobos could show the people who came there in August of each year what the hobo life was *really* like, that we could give them a better understanding of who the hobo was and what he had contributed to our nation's history.

I decided the best place to start was in constructing a proper hobo jungle and giving the visitors a chance to see and sample some authentic hobo cooking.

The chamber of commerce agreed to set aside a place for a jungle, and in 1972 I began with a small fire where I cooked some coffee and a pot of hobo stew which I made available to perhaps less than a hundred people. It was an immediate success and has since grown into a large cook fire with several huge pots feeding hundreds each year. The reaction I got from the city, from the visitors and from some of the other hobos was very encouraging and I began to think that perhaps I could do more if I became King of the Hobos.

The system used at the annual selection of the king was to allow candidates to spend several days politicking among the crowds who had come for the convention. Then, on election day, those who had decided to be candidates for the office would take their places on the stage and would be permitted to speak to the audience and to explain why they should be chosen for the honor of representing all hobos for the next year. Each candidate was given three minutes for his campaign address—although many would try to get at least five—after which the audience would, by their applause, select a king. A panel of judges would determine which candidate had received the most applause. Sometimes, when the voting was very close, it would take several rounds before the winner could be determined.

Some of the campaign speeches were quite grandiose and would have done some of the national presidential candidates proud for their eloquence and pomposity. But the best speech I ever heard a candidate give—and the briefest—was delivered by Slow-Motion Shorty who, after four or five long-winded orations from the other candidates, walked to the microphone and said, simply, "I'm the only hobo here who ever shook Leo Durocher's hand," and then turned and walked back to his seat. The applause for Shorty was overwhelming; he won the election by a landslide.

There had for many years been two hobos who had alternated each year being the national king; one of these was the Pennsylvania Kid. While I liked him, I felt he was a poor representative for all 'bos. He didn't have the dedication that I was always taught a true hobo should have, and he tended to be somewhat cruel and at times brutal. There were stories circulating around that the Kid had been known to use a knife when he found himself in a dispute with a "brother." The other hobo king was the Hard Rock Kid who, unlike the Pennsylvania Kid, enjoyed an excellent personal reputation and had many, many friends. But between them, the two seemed to have largely cornered the kingship and knew how to charm the audience into voting for them each year. It was very difficult to defeat them. Periodically another hobo would win against them—Slow-Motion was one—but most of the time they wore the crown.

Another thing I discovered was that whoever it was that won the title tended to do little with it other than to use it to get free drinks in bars and to stay drunk all year. (There were a number of imposters—mostly winos —who wandered around, stopping in beer joints and claiming to be King of the Hobos in order to get a couple of free rounds. I suspect there may be a few of those still left.)

I sincerely believed that a man who had been given what I considered the high honor of being chosen to represent the American hobo should do something worthwhile for the year he would serve, something more than simply enjoying the prestige and the publicity that came along with it.

Early in 1971, I had gone to Ann Arbor, Michigan, to visit an old friend who was in the veteran's hospital there. However, when I attempted to go inside, having just gotten off the train and looking pretty dirty in my hobo clothes, I was accosted by a security guard who refused to allow me beyond the lobby.

"I'm a veteran," I insisted, "and I can come in here anytime I want to. I'm here to see a friend and I'm going to see him."

After a lot of shouting and arguing, I guess they decided I wasn't going to be put off. Finally, the head of the security detail said that I would have to clean up first and then "get in and get out fast."

Some of the ambulatory patients in the lobby had heard the argument and, while I was washing up, spread out over the hospital telling the other patients about the "old hobo trying to get in."

After I had visited my friend some of the vets came up to me and asked if I would visit other floors. There wasn't a whole lot the administration could do at this point, so I was allowed access to other wards in the hospital. On one floor a nurse asked if I would see a man who had heard I was there and had asked to see me. "He's dying," the nurse said.

I went and sat by his bed, talking of what it was like being on the road and of some of the adventures I had experienced. He was thrilled by my visit and, while I still was at his bedside, he went into a coma and quietly slipped away.

The hospital was large and I couldn't get to everyone that day. But, by this time, word had reached just about everyone there and most hoped I could visit them. Many of these men—some whose service went back to the Spanish-American War—had been bedridden for decades, and almost all no longer received visits from family and friends. In the beginning, there had always been someone to call on them. But as the months and years passed, one by one the visits had dropped away and eventually no one came anymore. A visit from anyone, even a ragged old hobo, was a special treat. I couldn't deny them that small pleasure. I decided to stay over until the following day and see that anyone who wanted to talk to me had the opportunity.

The hospital had no place to house anyone but the patients—to have made a concession of that type would have opened the floodgates to all visitors and would have overtaxed their facility. However, they did allow me to sleep in the garage where they kept their lawn mowers and other maintenance equipment, which suited me just fine. They also fed me and saw to it that I had no further trouble with the security guards. I spent the next day completing my rounds of the full hospital.

Shortly after, the VA hospital in Allen Park, Michigan —a suburb of Detroit—heard about my visit and contacted me asking if I would visit the patients there. I spent two days visiting all the patients at the Allen Park facility.

When I decided to run for king, I knew exactly what I would do with the title if I won it.

In 1973 I campaigned for the first of what would be five runs for the hobo title.

"If I'm elected," I told the crowd of about 20,000 people, "I'll visit veterans' hospitals all over the country. If you elect me, you'll be sending me to those hospitals with your prayers for those men who have so little left to look forward to. They will be getting visits from *you*. They will be receiving *your* best wishes and *your* prayers."

I won easily.

I now had a mandate from all the people who had been there to carry a message of cheer to the men who had sacrificed so much for them.

I borrowed enough money to have 40,000 cards printed. On one side was my picture and the information that I was national king of the hobos. On the other was a message which stated: "Twenty thousand Americans have sent me to visit you. Their prayers and best wishes are on this card."

I began riding the freights to the various cities that had a veteran's hospital. I rode thousands of miles that year and walked hundreds of miles when there were no trains to ride. I had promised myself—and those who had elected me—that I would do nothing else that year but visit veterans. Near the end of the year, with time running out, I borrowed an additional three hundred dollars and bought a Greyhound "Ameripass," which allowed me to ride anywhere Greyhound went. I used it for three full months, riding and sleeping at night and visiting veterans during the day. In all, I made 34,000 bedside visits. And not the quick hello and hurry out kind of visit some of the vets told me celebrities made. I spent time talking to each of them, recounting my life on the iron road or talking about whatever they wanted to hear. I signed and distributed all of the 40,000 cards, with the balance going to doctors and nurses who asked to have one as a souvenir of my visit.

In 1973–1974, my first year as king, I visited one-third of all the veterans' hospitals in the U.S.

Being King of the Hobos opened the doors to these facilities. I not only had no trouble getting in, but when I was finished there would be invitations from two or three others waiting for me at the desk, all asking that I come to their hospital. I was invited to come to Walter Reed Hospital and, while there, was presented with a plaque, thanking me for my efforts on behalf of American veterans.

During that year I traveled through the Midwest from Chicago east to Maine, then down through New England, New York state, New Jersey and Pennsylvania. I visited Washington, D.C., Winston-Salem, North Carolina, Atlanta, Georgia—where I paid a visit to Governor George Wallace's office and presented one of my cards—and Montgomery, Alabama. I traveled through Mississippi, Louisiana, Texas, Oklahoma, New Mexico, then north as far as Boise, Idaho, then on to Cheyenne, Wyoming, which was the last stop before I had to break off my tour to make the hobo convention and surrender my crown—which, by the way, was made from an old coffee can.

Other than the meals the hospitals provided for me, I received nothing in financial compensation for my year traveling to visit the veterans. But I was paid royally in the satisfaction of knowing that I had done something worthwhile; the look in the eyes of those men, many of whom were so lonely, who felt forgotten and abandoned, gave me more joy than I could ever give them. The tears of gratitude they shed were matched by my own. I came away from those twelve months feeling that no matter what else I might do with my life I had done something I could be proud of. I had shown 34,000 men from five wars that they *are* remembered, that the sacrifice they made hasn't been ignored and that, while the debt we Americans owe them can never be marked "paid in full," at least some of those living outside their walls wanted them to know we still care, that we continue to acknowledge that debt.

There was one side-trip during that time that I fondly recall. After completing a visit to the Batavia, New York, VA hospital, the administrator asked if I would consider calling at the New York State School for the Blind, which was nearby.

"There are kids from all over the state there. I know your visit would mean a great deal to them."

I said I would be glad to go, if he could arrange it. He immediately got on the phone and set up my visit. They provided a car and took me to the school.

There were about 800 pupils at the school and I noticed, as they were filing into the auditorium, it was just like any other school, the same noises, the same rushing down the aisle to get the best seats. It was difficult, nearly impossible, for me to tell that these kids were sightless.

The principal introduced me: "The King of the Hobos is the only elected king in America and has a long white beard and looks like Santa Claus." They all laughed loudly.

I told them about the hobos, how they were naturalists who loved the outdoors and always worked for their food.

I told them of my love for the open country, describing forests and mountains and river banks, things that many had not seen in years and some had never seen at all . . . and probably never would.

They were one of the most attentive audiences I've spoken to, before or since.

When I had concluded my talk I asked for questions.

"How do you keep warm in the winter?" . . . "Are you afraid of animals?" . . . "Do you ever get lonely?" . . . "Could we be hobos?"

I answered each question as fully as I was able.

"I'm not afraid of animals; I respect them and treat them kindly. I've even had snakes come and lie down next to me to keep warm."—YUK!!—"I've never had any animals bother me, except the dog at your house, and even they can be nice."

The questions kept coming and the principal was growing uneasy.

"We've got to get back to our classes," he told them. "The bell has rung and we're getting behind in our work."

"Just one more question," the kids would shout, and then just one more.

Finally a girl stood up and said, "Just this last question."

"All right," he agreed. "But this has to be the last. We have to get back to our classes."

The girl asked:

"Can we come up and feel your beard?"

I laughed and said, "Sure, come on up."

They filed to the front of the auditorium where the principal guided each one to where I was. They put their hands on my shoulder and then up to my face.

Each would say, "Ooooh," and "Ahhhhh," and "It's soooo soft," and "What a wonderful Santa Claus."

They would each give the beard a little tug until I thought they might pull it all out.

As they finished moving their hands over my face, each

reached out and patted my arm or put their arms around me and gave me a hug.

I became so choked up, I thought my beard would become soaked in the tears that were streaming down my cheeks.

"I'm sorry we delayed you so long," the principal apologized later. "They were enjoying your visit so much they didn't want to let you get away. You were able to bring a world they've lost into their lives for a short time."

"Sir, I would have stayed until they threw me out."

And I meant it.

CHAPTER 16

THE REIGN OF "STEAM TRAIN"

Becoming the King of the Hobos produced an incredible alteration in my life. Prior to that event I had easily remained anonymous, unknown. And I liked it that way. Except for my wrestling successes I had always been a "nobody," a person who could move about freely, without fanfare. My unusual manner of dress might occasionally cause quizzical glances, a slight smile, a disapproving shake of the head. But I had never been sought out by the general public, never looked upon as someone special to be heralded as a celebrity, written about and photographed and quoted as an authority and an expert in any category of the human experience. Suddenly, all that changed and it was quite unsettling. I never wanted to be a celebrity, I wasn't schooled in that art and I think there were times when I didn't handle it all that well.

In previous years, the election of the national hobo king had been a light-hearted, humorous news item which the press treated as tongue-in-cheek and which the public had taken as insignificant and even slightly silly.

The earlier kings had viewed the title as having about as much importance as being named president of a fraternal lodge, whose worth was largely limited to gaining a few free drinks and perhaps a meal or two. Unlike Jeff Davis of the American Convention, who had attempted to benefit some segment of our society, the national hobo king had had no agenda for trying to contribute to our country.

As a result, the press—and the public—tended to ignore the hobo king once his election had been publicized. But my visits to VA hospitals offered the press a human interest angle that they couldn't turn down. TV cameras and the ever-present microphone shoved in my face became a regular part of my calls on the vets. The hospital administrators saw the value in reminding the public that there were many men who had served their country who had not and never would return to a normal place in society. And they understandably wanted to capitalize on my ability to attract attention.

Mixed in with my hospital visits were two experiences I never thought I'd ever have. The first was an invitation to appear on a very popular network TV game show called To Tell the Truth.

The format of the show was to bring three people before a panel of celebrities. Each of the three would claim to be the same individual and the panel was supposed to determine, through questioning, which was the authentic person, the one who was telling the truth.

Telling the truth didn't help me a great deal when I attempted to check into the Waldorf Astoria Hotel, where I'd been told I had a room reservation. I'd had enough trouble getting on the plane but that was nothing compared to what awaited me at the hotel in New York. Walking up to the hotel entrance, dressed in my hobo road outfit consisting of a ragged suit, battered old felt hat, a bedroll and bucket and a five-foot walking staff, the security guards who were employed to keep the street people and drifters out of the lobby seized me as soon as I got in the front door and dragged me back outside.

"Take your hands off me," I demanded. "I have a reservation in this hotel."

They looked at me as though I were insane; this ragged old bum insisting he had a room at the Waldorf Astoria.

I kept pulling away and trying to get back inside but every time I got near the door four guards would grab me and shove me back out on the sidewalk. I was about to start swinging when the chief of hotel security, having been alerted to the disturbance in front, came out to see what was going on.

"I've been trying to tell these dummies that I have a room in this hotel. You just go and check and you'll see. And if you don't get these goons off me, you're going to see more trouble than you ever imagined."

He took my name and started back inside, stopping just long enough to mutter to one of the guards: "I'll go and check and if he's lying, we'll beat the hell out of him."

A few minutes later he rushed back out, brushing at my clothes and taking my bindle.

"Open the door for this gentleman, and brush his clothes off."

I followed the security chief inside with guards tailing along behind, all trying to brush my clothes. For the next two days I couldn't open a door for myself; there was someone always around seeing to it that I wanted for nothing. I could have had anything—booze, a woman, tickets to hit Broadway shows. They tried their damnedest to make up for the hard time they'd given me.

On the TV show, Kitty Carlisle, one of the panelists, correctly picked me as the real hobo, although the other two appearing with me looked more like hobos than I did.

One was a high school teacher and the other taught piano.

In addition to all my expenses, I was awarded fifty dollars and a vacuum sweeper.

My second experience with celebrities proved especially enjoyable. This time I was one of ten guests of honor for a Hollywood premiere held in New York City. Twentieth Century-Fox had produced a movie entitled *Emperor of the North*, starring Lee Marvin and Ernest Borgnine. The plot involved a hobo (Marvin) riding the freights during the Depression and the efforts of a Union Pacific brakeman (Borgnine) to keep him off his train.

The publicity department for the studio contacted me and asked if I could supply ten authentic hobos—including myself—to attend the world premiere of the movie as their guests.

"Our budget is tight so we wouldn't be able to pay any of you," the PR man told me. "But you'll be flown to New York and put up at the Warwick Hotel; you'll be able to order anything you want to eat or drink; you'll attend the film's premiere with Lee Marvin and then join him later at a large banquet."

It sounded very elegant so I agreed. I got in touch with Slow-Motion Shorty, Hood River Blackie, Feather River John, Connecticut Slim and Bud Filer of the American Convention, and two others.

Shorty and I left together and almost didn't get on the plane. To begin with, we were both dressed in our tattered road clothes and carrying our bindles. The airline people weren't exactly thrilled to have two seedy-looking individuals boarding their plane. Then, I couldn't get through the security metal detector. Every time I walked through, buzzers and bells went off. I emptied my pockets and took every piece of metal off my suit and still the damned thing went off. People were lined up behind me and growing very impatient. The guards ran a hand-held detector over my body and nothing happened. But as soon as I stepped into the full-length machine it howled something awful. Finally, we discovered the problem; the metal eyelets on my ankle-length walking shoes had been causing the alarm to sound.

When we got to New York the PR man wanted to know where the other two hobos were.

"Eight was all I could come up with on short notice," I told him. "I thought it would be enough."

"Gee, we were really counting on ten; we've already sent out the publicity releases saying we would have that many. It wouldn't look too good if we couldn't deliver at least that many."

"Well," I said, "get me a car and I'll round up two more for you."

I began by touring the Bowery. I visited every mission I could find, inquiring of the men I found there if any had ridden the freights. But all I could come up with were winos who neither looked, smelled or acted like hobos. After a couple of hours of fruitless searching, knowing all the while that my pals were uptown having a good time, I decided that I would make one final try at the Salvation Army. I should have realized in the beginning that no self-respecting hobo would be in the missions—I myself never would. A hobo would head for the nearest Sally facility before going to a mission. Sure enough, I found two men who said that they had once ridden the trains but had fallen on hard times and had become winos.

"Where did you ride?" I asked, testing them before making an offer to take them uptown with me.

"I rode the Erie-Lackawana and the Pennsy," one told me. The other said he had mostly traveled the Rock Island west out of Chicago.

I asked some questions about hoboing and their answers satisfied me that they had indeed once ridden the freights.

"Come along with me and I'll show you one hell of a good time," I said, heading for the used clothing department where I outfitted them in proper hobo clothes to replace the filthy wino attire they had been wearing.

The schedule called for us to spend about a day and a half in New York. We were invited to meet Lee Marvin in his Waldorf Hotel room the next morning and then to have lunch with him. He and I would also be taking a stroll up Fifth Avenue for newspaper publicity photos. Finally, we would all go to the premiere and then to a banquet in the Waldorf's Louis XVI room. It was all pretty heady stuff for a bunch of guys who usually ate out of tin cans and slept in empty boxcars or under bridges.

We discovered that the PR man the studio had assigned to us was a penny-pinching miser who, I thought, was holding down expenses so he could keep the studio's bankroll for himself. He took us to the Warwick's dining room for dinner the first night. When the waitress came to our table, he ordered eighteen-dollar surf and turf for himself and seven-dollar hamburger steaks for us.

"Wait a minute," I shouted. "We know how to read a menu; we'll order our own meal."

When the waitress asked if we would like a drink before dinner, the PR man said, "No, we won't be having anything to drink."

Again I interrupted.

"Yes, we will; we ALL want drinks."

The PR man panicked.

"You're going to be meeting a lot of important people. You've got to stay sober for the next two days; you can't be drunk."

"YOU can't be drunk, but WE can. We'll have several drinks before we eat."

That first evening in New York had no planned events so we all went down to the bar and badgered the studio man to buy drinks, which proved to be no easy task. However, through firm intimidation we managed to make an evening of it.

Shorty, who was a confirmed baseball nut, decided he

would take the subway to the Bronx and see a Yankee's game. He had mentioned his wish earlier in the afternoon and a studio executive had heard about it and provided him with a season pass to the company's expensive box seats. He knew his way around New York, having been there many times. So off he went, all alone.

About four hours later, just when I was beginning to be concerned about him, Shorty staggered into the bar, his arms entwined with those of a very important-looking gentleman. The two gave the impression of being lifelong friends, and I couldn't imagine where or how he had come across someone of such obvious breeding and social status. They joined us at our table and, after a few fumbled attempts at introductions, Shorty explained the circumstances which had led him to make this new "friend for life."

Sitting in the highest-priced section of the stadium caused a stir among the other people in those seats. A man in the next box, probably curious about this unkempt individual sitting where he obviously had no right to be, engaged Shorty in conversation. Within a few minutes Shorty had thoroughly charmed the stranger and was regaling him with stories of his hobo experiences. The fellow turned out to be a very wealthy businessman who found the little hobo to be absolutely enchanting. The man had a fifth of whiskey with him and invited Shorty to join him in a drink or two. By the time the game was over, the two were fast friends.

As he was walking down the cement stairway after the game, Shorty—perhaps from too much expensive bourbon—tripped and tumbled the full length of the staircase, ripping his clothes and causing a huge, ugly-looking bruise on his back.

"Look, my friend. I have a limousine out front. Let me take you back to your hotel," his new-found benefactor suggested.

He did and spent the balance of the evening in the hotel

bar, surrounded by ten hobos. It was undoubtedly the most unusual evening he'd spent in his life.

The next morning I was taken over to meet Lee Marvin. We sat in the suite he and his wife shared and spent a couple of hours in friendly conversation. I found him to be a very pleasant, polite man; I liked him right away. Unfortunately, Ernest Borgnine wasn't able to be in New York for the premiere and I was sorry I didn't get a chance to meet him as well.

At lunch, Marvin asked me:

"Are they taking good care of you fellows?"

"Hell no!" I replied. "That guy holding the money won't spend nothing. We're not getting paid for this but they told us we could have anything we want to eat and drink. But that guy's squeezing every nickel in his pocket."

Marvin's jaw tensed up and his eyes got real narrow. He called the studio man over and chewed him out something fearful.

"You will get these guys anything they want. Do you understand, anything they want."

From the look on his face, I thought he might grab him by the throat.

"Oh, sure, Mr. Marvin," the flunky said, trembling a little and starting to sweat.

"I'll be checking on you; if I hear that you're not treating these men right, I'll come looking for you, and you can believe that!"

That night we attended the premiere which I found most enjoyable. At the banquet afterwards I gave Marvin a quick education in hobo history in general and about the man he'd played in particular. He was quite surprised that the movie had been based on two actual characters, A-Number One, the Rambler, and his sidekick, a man called Cigarette.

"I never knew much about hobos," he admitted. "Although I always thought I probably should have been one."

He sat with us throughout the evening, ordering drinks all around and seemingly having a good time. The PR man cornered me when I went to the men's room and practically pleaded with me to keep Marvin from drinking too much.

"We have to meet the press tomorrow. Don't let him get started on the booze or he'll drink all night."

"Now, don't you worry, friend," I assured him, patting him on the chest. "We'll keep up with him."

The two men I'd recruited at the Salvation Army didn't seem to be enjoying themselves, so I took them aside and told them that they could have anything they wanted.

"You won't be getting paid for this," I said. "So you might as well drink whatever you like. Order anything from the top shelf, the most expensive whiskey."

"Well, as I told you," one of them said. "We're just a couple of winos. We're not used to that fancy stuff anymore."

"Well, you can have anything you want. What would you like?"

They replied in unison.

"Muscatel."

And not just any muscatel, but the cheapest skid row, seventy-nine cent a bottle rotgut that was often called "white puke."

I called the wine steward over and told him what the two wanted. He turned pale and I thought he would fall over. In barely disguised indignation, he informed me that such inferior wine had no place in his cellar.

"Well, that's what my friends here want. So I'd suggest you send someone out to the cheap bars and locate some. And make sure you get enough so they can take a couple of bottles with them."

• • •

As the 1973–1974 King of the Hobos there was one obligation I felt duty bound to attend to.

With the planned phasing out of the railroads had

come a severe personnel cutback. The once-despised railroad bulls had been reduced to an ineffective few who were powerless to halt the growing larceny of freight cars. The thieves were becoming so bold, they were backing large trucks up to the boxcars in broad daylight and carrying away the entire contents.

An extreme danger to hobos resulted; the thieves, seeing a hobo wandering into the yards and fearing he would identify them, would fall upon him, beating him mercilessly and frequently killing him. Simply because he happened to be in the vicinity, the 'bo had become a target, a victim whose life was the price he paid for being there.

I firmly believed that something should be done to stop the assaults on my hobos, that the railroads had to rehire the guards and that the government should assist in this project. I'd heard that there was a bill in Congress to provide several million dollars to bring back some of the railroad police and to beef up rail yard security. However, the bill was stalled in committee and there was little hope that it would be reported out during that session. I decided that I should do whatever I could to get the wheels turning again.

My sister Alice had once worked for a family of wealthy ranch owners in Idaho named Symms. She had practically raised one of the Symms children, a boy named Steven. By 1973, Steve had been elected to the U.S. House of Representatives from Idaho. I felt he might be a worthwhile contact in my efforts to get legislation passed to provide for more railroad guards.

When I came through Washington on my VA hospital tour I took the opportunity to call at his office. His secretary was very polite when I first walked in, even though I gave her quite a start, dressed as I was in my hobo clothes. I could tell that her first reaction to me was of unease, thinking that she may be facing some kind of looney.

"I'm sorry, but Representative Symms is on the floor of

the House at present," she told me when I asked to see him. "Actually, his appointment schedule is booked several months in advance. If you wish, I can try to schedule you for later this year."

"I'm afraid I don't have that much time," I explained. "But I have something very important that I want to talk to him about."

She was unsympathetic, probably wanting to get rid of me as fast as possible. Then I mentioned that Alice knew the family very well and had taken care of the congressman when he was just a baby. I mentioned that I knew the family, too.

"Are you from Idaho?" she asked.

I told her that I had lived there and that most of my family had settled there, and that Alice and her husband continued to be residents of Idaho.

Her attitude softened and when I explained that I was National King of the Hobos, the atmosphere warmed noticeably. Within minutes the office staff had surrounded me and I was signing and passing out some of the cards I carried.

"I'm going into the chamber to speak to Mr. Symms," the secretary explained. "Why don't you come along with me?"

We went down to the lobby of the House and I waited outside while she went in to talk to Symms. Soon she returned and told me that he had asked that I be taken to the gallery to wait until the session was finished. He would speak to me then. She said that he remembered Alice very well and was anxious to meet with me.

I was ushered to the front row of the gallery where I stood, peering down into the well of the House looking for Symms, my long beard hanging over the rail. Steve glanced up, saw me and waved lightly. The man seated next to him looked up, saw this strange apparition with the weird clothes and the long white beard waving down at him, and waved, too. The the man next to him looked up and waved.

On one side of the chamber a representative was giving a very forceful speech, shouting and banging on his desk with his fist.

As I stood waving down at the congressmen, one by one each, noticing the person next to him looking up to the gallery and waving, looked upward himself and, seeing me standing up there like I was the pope waving at the multitude, waved back at me. It moved like the "wave" in a sports stadium from one member of the House to the next, each turning, looking up and waving. As the wave spread across the room, the members suddenly began to chuckle at the sight. The chuckle grew until it was full-blown laughter and still the waving continued.

The member who had been busily engaged in his impassioned speech was the only one unaware of what was happening. Suddenly taking notice of the growing laughter, he looked up from his notes and fist-banging, saw the object of the House's attention and laughter, threw up his hands and proclaimed: "Hell, I might as well wave, too. Nobody's listening to what I have to say."

The member in the Speaker of the House's chair (I'm not certain if it was the Speaker himself) gaveled the chamber to order and demanded that the session continue undisturbed by the gallery audience.

When the session had been adjourned, Steve came out and greeted me warmly. We returned to his office and after a few minutes' talk about "the old days" in Idaho and about Alice, I told the representative, "I came to see you about a matter that needs immediate attention. The nation can't wait."

I then went into a detailed explanation of what was happening to our country's railroad system and particularly what the effect was on the freight yards and the millions of dollars in property that was being stolen and the physical threat the loss of adequate security posed to anyone venturing into the yards.

"You've got to get that bill out and voted on. This is hurting my hobos," I told him.

The congressman was not only sympathetic to my concerns but was understanding of the impact it could have on the nation. He asked me to meet with the other congressmen, and during the balance of that day I spoke with six or seven other members of the House.

My visit to the House and the disruption I'd caused did not escape the notice of the press. That night a national television anchorman reported how one of the congressional newspaper correspondents had telephoned his editor and told him that there had "been a bum in congress" that day.

"What's so newsworthy about that?" the editor wanted to know. "The place is full of bums."

I had to leave the next morning and couldn't be in Washington to follow up on the legislation. But, through newspaper accounts, I learned that within a week the bill had been reported out and was immediately passed. The money was appropriated and the bulls were hired back. I felt very good: I had done something important for the hobos; I had contributed something to the country; and I had been instrumental in getting the bulls their jobs back.

Unfortunately for me, within a few months the railroad police were kicking the hell out of me for riding the freights. I couldn't tell them that I had gotten their jobs back for them, I knew they'd just laugh at me.

Steven Symms moved up in his political career and is now a U.S. senator. The people of Idaho apparently recognized his contributions to the state.

• • •

I had spent an exhausting year traveling and looked forward to some quiet hoboing, returning to peaceful anonymity. But that wasn't to be. The publicity I'd received because of my visits to veteran's hospitals, my appearance on television and the news accounts and photos of me and Lee Marvin had given me an unwelcome celebrity. I was suddenly in demand for a variety of personal appearances all over the country. A constantly growing number of railroad festivals were cropping up and invitations began catching up with me on the road, asking that I come to lead their parade or speak before some group. I was invited by a number of chambers of commerce to address their memberships, by various fraternal and professional organizations, church groups, Boy Scouts, and just about everyone who had planned a function and was looking for an unusual attraction to heighten public awareness and interest in their project. I was almost never offered any fee or honorarium for my time and trouble and I never asked for such. I had no expenses in traveling to these gatherings—as long as I could find an open boxcar or a willing motorist to heed my outstretched thumb.

Probably the strangest invitation I was to receive during the years that followed my first election as hobo king was a request that I appear as "Special Guest" at the fifth annual "Miss Maryland Teen-ager State Finals" in 1976. What possible connection I had with a teen-age beauty contest has always escaped me. But I accepted the invitation and participated. Everyone seemed delighted to have me take part in their pageant. The girls were very charming, polite and attentive and I had a thoroughly pleasant time.

In my travels to the various events to which I had been invited, I managed to do a bit of old-time hoboing, hooking up several times with Fry Pan Jack and Slow-Motion Shorty. But it was becoming increasingly difficult to live the hobo life. The railroad continued in decline, the old short lines had disappeared and the mainlines didn't have the traffic anymore.

In the mid-1970s a very low character type was traveling the road, heavily into dope, ready and willing to steal anything that could be sold for another fix or a few joints. Dope and crime go hand in hand. As narcotics use spread over the country, larceny, muggings and murder spread along with it. Old hobos were easy marks for the dangerous types roaming the road. Many of the old-time hobos called it quits, put the road behind them forever or became "rubber tire hobos" with campers and motor homes. Yet, with the growing disappearance of the hobo there came a greater appreciation of what he had been and the historic place he had occupied in our country's development.

In 1974 I received a letter from Inmate Number 87047-132, a young man who was serving twenty-five *and* fifty-year concurrent sentences in Leavenworth Federal Penitentiary for a pair of Texas bank robberies. It was such a plaintive letter that I had to respond. From that grew a close friendship that has endured for more than fourteen years.

His name was Rick Sikes, a high-school dropout who had spent his young adult years "fighting and raising hell," on drugs and booze and bad company. Rick had been a member of a small band that played everything from country and western music to rock. While in prison he had continued with his music, become a talented artist in ceramics as well as in pen and ink sketching. He had earned his high-school diploma and begun writing poetry and composing songs. He had decided to make something of himself, but received little support from the prison administration.

"Prison officials' attitudes are mostly paranoid and doubtful of any self-inspired projects of inmates," he said, "and not entirely without reason. They have been tricked every possible way."

But having done nothing with his life before prison to make himself feel proud, he became determined to walk a different road.

"I decided that I'd messed up all those years and might as well try something different," he said.

An assistant warden named Dudley Blevins found in Rick's music a promise of something good inside Rick and used his influence to have a prison room set aside for music. The room eventually became a recording studio designed and constructed by inmates using egg cartons glued to the walls for soundproofing and a mixing board made from spare parts they were able to round up.

In one of his letters, Rick asked me to visit him the next time I came through Kansas. I agreed and between us we arranged for the necessary clearance to have me added to his visitor's list. The first time I walked up to that forbidding front gate was an awesome experience, and going behind those cold, grey walls filled me with apprehension and depression.

The prison's program director had learned that the King of the Hobos was coming to Leavenworth and met me in the waiting room.

"After your visit with Rick, I wonder if you would consider speaking to the general prison population?" he asked.

I said I'd be happy to, and later I was taken to the auditorium, where those who wished to could come in and listen to me talk about my life as a hobo. We had a question and answer period afterwards. I fully expected they would want to hear about women and nightclubs and the earthy things on the outside that were totally denied them. Instead they asked about fishing on a creek bank and about flowers and nature. They wanted to talk about woods, rivers, trees and traveling over the country and visiting with people.

One old man who had been there for many years said: "My biggest dream is to go to a woods and find the tallest tree. I'd climb up to the very top and sit there and sway back and forth all day long."

They all treated me very well; they seemed so happy that I had come there and had agreed to talk with them. As I was preparing to leave, the warden asked where I was staying. I told him I had spent the previous night in the woods by the river.

"Whenever you come here again, check into the motel a block up the street. Tell them you're my guest and to send me the bill," he told me.

It was called the Federal Motel and people who came to visit prisoners would stay there. But I was the only one—as far as I knew—who was a guest of the prison warden.

My visit to Leavenworth began another of my projects as hobo king and was the first of many stops there and at two other Federal prisons: the federal facility in Ashland, Kentucky, and the one at Milan, Michigan. I have also been invited to the Federal Penitentiary at Lewisburg, Pennsylvania, but, as yet, haven't gotten there. But I visited Leavenworth four years in a row and became the only nonemployee who could walk up to the gates and be admitted and allowed into the mess hall with the men.

At one of the Britt conventions I met a musician from Kansas City named Don Hupp. He had a very fine bluegrass group called the Great White Possum String Band. He was a wonderful, caring fellow and I asked him to bring his band to Leavenworth when I visited the next time. Don agreed immediately and the band went in with me several times thereafter, much to the delight of the prisoners. When the program director asked me to visit the Milan prison, I took a bluegrass group from Toledo with me three years straight.

Rick Sikes, after serving fourteen years of his sentence, was paroled on August 16, 1985. He now lives in Coleman, Texas, where he reports to two parole officers—one federal and one state. He recently opened a small recording studio in partnership with several others who believe in his music, his abilities and his character. I was honored to be invited to the grand opening and happily attended. Rick has become a "friend for life."

• • •

Because I felt there had been problems created by one or two men monopolizing the hobo title in the past, I decided that I would not run for king again for at least two years. Actually, I waited for three before launching my second campaign in 1976.

My strategy at the convention that year was to spend the two days before the election moving around town, ingratiating myself with senior citizens and children, asking the children to urge their parents to vote for me. The strategy worked and I was elected for my second term as National King of the Hobos.

With my second term as king came an increasing number of invitations to attend community programs and several additional offers to appear on national television. I also began hearing from a wide range of private citizens who sought to contact me and to initiate a correspondence and a friendship with me simply because I was a hobo.

In addition to my visits to prisons I determined that I would continue my "reign" by attempting to educate the American people about the hobo and the historic treasure he had become. I became more successful than I ever dreamed I would: not only did many people in the U.S. become familiar with my name and face in their local newspapers and on local television, but a few people in other countries did, too. As one result, I have maintained a twelve-year correspondence with a man in Australia, who has become as close to me as a brother.

I was also to be of some interest to producers of national television programs. In the mid-1970s a fellow named Tom Snyder had a late night talk show on NBC. It was called the *Tomorrow Show* and it followed Johnny Carson each night. I was asked to appear with Snyder and was flown to Los Angeles to be on the show. After getting off the plane in L.A., dressed as usual in my full hobo road clothes, I was walking through the concourse on my way to the baggage area where I was told to meet the limousine driver NBC would send. There was a light stream of people walking in my direction with about the same number heading toward the boarding gate I had just come from. Ahead, walking in my direction, I saw Charles Bronson. I was intrigued at seeing this ultra-famous person in the flesh and couldn't take my eyes off him. At about the same moment he noticed me, probably equally intrigued by this strange-looking dude with the white beard, slouch hat and old clothes covered with buttons and badges, carrying a bedroll and an eight-gallon can (which I always took with me to serve as a suitcase and a comfortable seat if I had to sit down for a while) and old walking boots held on by huge rubber bands. All the while we were approaching, we kept our eyes locked on each other and as we passed our heads turned in unison and we continued to eye one another down the long corridor. Finally, just before he went out of sight, Bronson smiled, then laughed loudly and waved.

In the baggage claim area I waited until I saw this tall man with a chauffeur's hat moving in my direction and calling for "Mr. Graham! Mr. Graham!" But if he was surprised to have me step forward and acknowledge that I was the one he sought, the people there were astonished. This ragged old bum, carrying all that junk, being met by a fancy limousine and driver was more than they were prepared for. As we went outside and got into the car the unbelieving crowd continued to stare. The driver was pulling away when he called my attention to the huge glass wall that ran all along the drive. The crowd had moved to the windows and, almost with their noses pressed against the panes, they were still watching me, wondering who in the hell I could be.

"Since I started this job," the driver said as we drove away, "I've picked up senators and congressmen, movie and television stars, rock and roll singers, princes and princesses, and I can tell you *no one* has created the kind of fuss that you just caused."

We both laughed.

The Snyder interview went very well, and he proved to be a perfect gentleman and an excellent host who made me feel very comfortable and welcome.

• • •

I continued to travel, attending railroad festivals, visiting prisons, speaking before school groups and calling on senior citizens.

I ran for another term as king in 1978, planning not to run again for at least two more years. But near the end of that term I learned that two nonhobos had announced their intentions to run for the title. One was a bartender from a town near Britt who had decided that it might be "fun to go on over there and become a king." The other man was a fellow who planned to write a book and thought that the title would help him sell it. I just couldn't stand the thought of a phony becoming hobo king. To keep this from happening I decided I would, as the incumbent king, have a better chance of beating these two frauds. And I did. I announced that I would run for another term in order to "keep these two fellows, who never rode a freight train in their lives," from spoiling the office of king of the hobos. I won by a landslide.

There were fewer and fewer of the old hobos left. When I went back on the road in 1971 there were about 300 still traveling in various parts of the country, mostly the Midwest and the West Coast. When I went east I discovered I was the only hobo still riding the freights in that part of the country.

The loss of the railroads and the passage of time were slowly winnowing away our once large and proud group. Word was reaching me with a mournful regularity of the loss of yet another old-time 'bo. The Westbound was running a stepped-up schedule, and the friends I had developed over a fifty-year period were rushing to catch it.

CHAPTER 17

A DRINK OF WHISKEY ON HIS GRAVE

In the small cemetery in Lamont, Iowa, where the unknown hobo was buried, lies another nameless 'bo. No one knows exactly where in the cemetery his grave is located. Apparently there were no young girls like those who placed a stone marker over the unknown hobo's head, to feel concern for this lonesome old wanderer.

Whoever he was, he perhaps best typifies those who have caught the westbound, who had nobody to mourn their leaving or to want to memorialize their lives.

For more than a hundred years hobos died on the road, their bodies frequently buried along the trackside, hurriedly interred with nothing more than a crude pile of stones to mark their graves. Occasionally, brother hobos would attempt to conduct a "proper funeral." The departed would be wrapped in his blanket, maybe his personal possessions would be tenderly placed on his chest, while one of the attending hobos would read from a small Bible he carried with him or, as was most often the case, recite from memory an appropriate verse while another with a harmonica played a soft and tender dirge.

But most often, the departed 'bo was buried by whichever "authorities" happened to find him. Sometimes he was placed in the local "Potter's Field," sometimes—when his remains were discovered along the railroad right-of-way, far from a settlement of any size—he was simply "planted" in the most convenient hole or depression. There was no marker, no cross or tablet, his name was not etched in stone nor chalked on a board. He was disposed of, gotten rid of.

In the 1920s and 1930s hundreds—perhaps thousands—of hobos and other travelers were killed trying to get on or off trains or were pushed from speeding trains by railroad bulls or train crews, or were shot and killed around rail yards and aboard the freights. Many of these were buried without ceremony and without love. Only a few, such as Lamont's unknown hobo, were treated with tenderness by sympathetic townspeople who believed that even a hobo was entitled to a Christian burial.

In 1977, what promises to be a tradition began with the burial of the Hard Rock Kid in Britt's Evergreen Cemetery.

The Kid was much loved throughout Iowa, his traveling circuit. Wherever he went in the state he was welcomed with open arms. Probably his favorite town was Ogden, Iowa, a tiny community about ninety miles south of Britt. On July 24, 1977, the Kid was slowly making his way toward Britt for the annual convention. He had stopped in Ogden and, as was his custom, had declined offers to "come inside and take a nap," preferring instead to stretch out under a shade tree in the city park.

It was late in the afternoon when a local police officer stopped at the park to check on the Kid. Out under his beloved open sky the Kid, in his seventy-second year, had caught the Westbound. A search could locate no relatives, but then he didn't need any; he had countless friends who would mourn him.

It was decided he should be allowed to continue his journey to Britt and be buried there, in the place where five times he had been chosen king of the hobos. Four of his hobo friends, Virginia Slim, Sparky Smith, Fry Pan and myself went to Ogden to bring him to Britt.

The people of Ogden wanted to hold a memorial service for him before we took him away. Bob Carson's funeral home was selected as the site. The place was not very large, but the funeral home staff felt that it would be adequate for the thirty or forty they believed would want to attend. They should have known better. Several hundred showed up, filled the funeral home and spilled out on the lawn in front. As the organist played "King of the Road," I was given the honor of delivering the eulogy.

"The Kid had more friends in the state than anyone living," I said. "Everywhere I go, people say they saw him. There isn't a town or a hamlet or a crossroads in this state where he hasn't stayed. That was his home. You were his home, his friends."

Later, in Britt, where more than two hundred people crowded into the cemetery, Father John J. Brickley, the local Catholic priest and the Hobos' Chaplain, conducted a graveside service in a quiet spot in the shade of the trees he loved and not more than a hundred feet from the railroad tracks where he so often used to jump aboard a passing freight train. I was again asked to say something about the Kid and again I commented on his love for Iowa.

"It was his home. Any common road, any city, any hamlet in this state was his home. Who could forbid him from falling asleep the way he did in the open, dying under a tree? He'd rather sleep under the stars than anywhere else. The governor didn't know as many men as this man did. He's still lying close to his tracks. He's still riding."

On his casket I placed a red bandana I had worn on dozens of trips on the freights and, raising my walking stick, said: "We bid you Godspeed."

The red bandana was a part of the hobo uniform, worn for the same purpose that railroad crewmen always sported such neckwear: to keep hot cinders and ash from steam engines from getting down inside the collar and burning the victim. A red bandana is always buried with a hobo to protect him from the hot sparks of the Westbound.

As thunder from an approaching summer rainstorm rumbled in the distance, those attending the service walked slowly by, tossing clumps of earth down into the open grave.

Father John is a man of compassion, sensitivity, concern and dedication, with a genuine love for all hobos, whatever their religious affiliation. A slight, balding man, he looks like a very prim and proper servant of his Church, one who would not take kindly to the itinerants who flocked to Britt to engage in a weekend of revelry. Father John simply does not look like the picture of a priest who would be unusually concerned about the welfare of a bunch of hobos who can do little if anything for his parish and who do not fit the mold of a God-fearing Christian. Yet, over an eighteen-year period, Father John was always available to the hobos who came through Britt or who appeared for the annual convention. He conducts the memorial service we hold the day before the convention each year, and he has always been there to conduct the burial service for those who've caught the Westbound and wished to find their final resting place in the small cemetery in Britt.

Father Brickley is retired now. Yet he is kept very busy, traveling to other parts of the country to substitute or to give additional assistance to parishes needing help. A telephone call to his residence will frequently provide the caller with little more than a recorded message announcing that he is not available at the moment, but if there is a *real* emergency, the caller can contact the Ewing funeral home to learn where he can be reached.

I believe Father John lives by Christ's caveat that "what ye do unto the least of these ye do also unto Me." A large number of the remaining hobos have indicated that they want Father John to conduct their burial ceremonies. I certainly would be honored if he conducted mine. I truly hope he will be there for me when the time comes.

• • •

In April, 1984, after a long, bitter struggle with cancer, Charles "Mountain Dew" Troxel died in the veteran's hospital in Minneapolis, Minnesota. He was 61.

Mountain Dew had asked that he be buried in Evergreen Cemetery near the Hard Rock Kid's grave. Roger Ewing of the Carter-Ewing Funeral Chapel donated his time to arrange for the burial, the Wilbert Vault Company and Mastercraft Casket Company donated a burial vault and a casket and a plot, near the Hard Rock Kid, was provided at no charge by the cemetery.

I was not contacted in time to be at the funeral, but Sparky Smith and Virginia Slim were able to get to Britt in time for the ceremony. A number of us, including Fry Pan Jack, Gallway Slim and I were named as honorary pallbearers, and a red bandana was placed on Dew's coffin as it was lowered into the grave. He was buried in his colors and patches and hobo clothes.

Dew had not let his battle with cancer keep him from riding freights, not until he became too ill to travel. The previous August he had come to Britt for the convention and had run and been elected king. He was very pleased at the honor and his hobo pals were happy for him because we knew his time was running out.

Mountain Dew became the second consecutive hobo king to not live through his term of office. M. L. "Hobo Bill" Mainer, the reigning king in 1983, had died part way through his term.

The third hobo to go to his final rest in Britt was for me the greatest loss of all.

In the early morning hours of May 23, 1985, the brave heart of Albert William Parker ceased to beat. Slow-Motion Shorty had caught the Westbound. For me, the low, throaty moan of those few steam locomotive whistles that remain will have a more mournful cry from now on.

Even in death, Shorty did not forget his brother 'bos, nor the quiet little town that had always been a second home. After his death it was discovered that he had somehow accumulated 3,000 dollars in traveler's checks and a small checking account. It was probably the most money he had ever had at one time in all of his sixty-nine years. A handwritten will was found among his personal effects. In it he stated that he had never married and had no living relatives. He directed that 500 dollars from his estate be given to the Sacramento, California, senior citizens' home where he had spent the final four years of his life. He asked that the remaining 2500 dollars be given to the city of Britt to be used to help fund the annual hobo convention. He also asked that his ashes be buried in Evergreen Cemetery—on Hobo Row.

In between the deaths of Hard Rock Kid and Slow-Motion Shorty, we lost many hobos, among them Lord Open Road—who was murdered by muggers for the three dollars in his pockets—Hood River Blackie, "Ole the 'Bo" Mills, "Bigtown" Gorman and the Cheyenne Kid. The list of old hobos I've known who have caught the Westbound grows each year.

Ben "Scoop Shovel" Benson is gone, "Lying Roy" Livingston was run down and killed by a car in 1969, Bill Sondell was stoned to death by a gang of teenagers in Washington, and "Mule Train" Smith vanished from a train in Idaho in 1968. Parnell "Chicken Red" Donovan, who spent over seventy years on the road, The Panama Kid, Mainline John, Lead Belly and Cache Junction Whitey—all are gone.

Unintentionally, we caused a minor controversy at the Hard Rock Kid's funeral.

Before he died, the Kid had asked that someone pour "a drink of whiskey" into his grave. Since it was his last request we brought a bottle of Irish whiskey to the cemetery and, after the jug was passed to each of the hobos who took a swig, a hearty drink was poured into his grave.

Later, several Britt citizens bitterly complained to me:

"We don't like the idea of bringing liquor into the cemetery. We have loved ones buried there and we don't think it's very Christian of you to treat this hallowed ground that way."

I explained, as courteously as I could, that we meant no disrespect to anyone but were only fulfilling the Kid's last wish.

When Mountain Dew was buried, we poured soda pop in his grave, again at his request. Dew had never consumed alcoholic beverages. At Slow-Motion Shorty's burial we poured water into his grave, although, on reflection, we might have dropped in some wine; Shorty had been known, in earlier years, to enjoy a bit of the grape.

Many of the remaining old hobos have indicated their desire to be buried in the Britt cemetery. Liz Lump, the black hobo queen, has already purchased a plot for herself in Evergreen Cemetery.

I would like to be buried there. However, Wanda insists that my place is next to her in Toledo. Perhaps she would agree to having me cremated and sending a coffee can with some of my ashes to Britt.

The old hobos are drifting away and there are not a lot of young ones to take their place. In California, two enterprising young men named Bob Hopkins and Garth Bishop have formed the National Hobo Association which publishes a newsletter known as the *Hobo Times.* The express purpose of the newsletter, according to Hopkins, is to raise money for "indigent travelers." Hopkins also hopes to inspire a greater interest in and understanding of the hobo.

Hopkins, a part-time television actor, has more than an intellectual acquaintance with hoboing, having ridden freights for about ten years. His first experience with the iron road came when he was in his twenties, was unemployed, and wanted to get from Los Angeles to Boston to celebrate his grandfather's ninetieth birthday. It took thirteen trains and eight days but he was hopelessly hooked on no-ticket travel. He later took his brother and brother-in-law to Las Vegas and later made a television documentary called "The Great American Hobo" which was shown on PBS in 1981.

Hopkins said that he believes the life of the hobo appeals to the office-bound city dweller who envies a life of no schedules, no bank accounts, no family responsibilities and, most of all, no pressure. He speaks warmly of being aboard a boxcar where "you sit back and look out this big huge open door. It's like a movie . . . you see herds of wild mustangs . . . a lot of stuff you don't see along the highways . . ."

According to Hopkins there are California groups of young professional people who enjoy a form of weekend hoboing.

It is not likely that the hobo will survive modern America; there are just too many obstacles. But there are indications that the hobo lore and the mystique that has grown around the hobo will not only continue but may possibly grow.

In the meantime, the handful of us that survive will go on bringing our hobo message of conservation of the precious resources we possess and of the love and dedication we have always had toward mankind. Perhaps the life the hobo has sought to live can become a guidepost to future generations. If that can be done, the hobo will have made a valuable and worthwhile contribution to society.

CHAPTER 18

TIRED OF RUNNING THE LINE

There is a certain type of man who cannot be content to stay in one place for a lifetime, a man who must always know what is over the horizon: he must travel. He is part of a minority of nomads who have a persistent itch to visit unknown places. The poet Robert Service wrote of the race of men "who don't fit in." They were vagabonds, men who could not abide confinement. They had to be free of regimentation and restriction; men who had no allegiance to regulated society. They could not spend all their lives in the hungry pursuit of material possessions, striving for promotions and status. They wished to be unfettered, free from the bounds that society imposes on those it will accept. For more than a century they roamed the nation, calling no place home, having no place where they were required to be, living in the open, tuned to nature. The hobo was this type. I was this type.

There were those—most people, in fact—who looked with scorn on the hobo. They believed he was no different than the bum, and they referred to all vagabonds with this derisive term. To them, all wanderers were irresponsible misfits who contributed nothing to the rest of the society; to them, wanderers were unwilling, and perhaps unable, to take a worthwhile, productive place in the world. The hobo didn't fit the mold that has been fashioned for "acceptable behavior."

I began to better understand this attitude when I first assumed the title of National Hobo King, and I sought to do as much as I could to dispel what I believed to be an incorrect and potentially destructive view; I wanted everyone to truly understand who the hobo was, what drove him. I had successfully campaigned for the role of king four times by 1980—I would run and win once more—and during that period I began to feel what I believed was a definite change in the attitude of the public.

There had always been those who appreciated and even loved the hobo, and it was encouraging to see that the number seemed to be growing even as the numbers of old-time hobos were shrinking. There was a warmer attitude wherever I went. The pleasant kindness and consideration that people were extending to me was most gratifying.

Here are but a few examples of the generosity and sensitivity I experienced from some of those I met.

Once, when I was in Marshalltown, Iowa, a brakeman in the yards there saw me getting ready to run for a moving train. He stopped me and said, "The next one will be coming through in just a little while. It will be stopping here. You won't have to catch it on the fly. Why don't you wait for that one?"

I was in no big hurry, so I thanked him for being so considerate and helpful and waited. That first train got six miles out of town and left the tracks; the cars were all piled up and some of them caught fire. That brakeman probably saved my life.

. . .

During a trip to Tennessee I met Larry Eddins who, at that time, was water commissioner in Fayetteville. I'd got to talking to Larry in a bar and, after an hour or two, he invited me to have dinner with him that night. A strong friendship grew out of that chance meeting and whenever I was in Fayetteville I called him. He was always happy to see me but he never invited me to his home. It took a couple of years before he finally admitted to me that his wife Elizabeth had refused to allow him to bring "an old bum" into their home and cause her embarrassment among the bluenoses of the neighborhood.

I understood her concerns and it didn't interfere with my friendship with Larry. Finally, however, I was surprised one day during a visit to Fayetteville when Elizabeth called Larry at his office and told him to invite me up to the house. We had an extremely pleasant visit and I apparently won Elizabeth over because I was always welcome in their home after that. She was a teacher in the local school and even asked me to speak before one of her classes. Of course, I was delighted to do so. When their son Dennis was installed as an Eagle Scout, they invited me to come down for the ceremonies. It was a very proud moment for me.

Larry eventually became very ill and through many long, burning months I awaited the dreaded notice of his demise. And, indeed, the notice came one day but, oddly, his passing was as the result of a traffic accident rather than from his terminal illness. I still correspond with Elizabeth and Dennis and stop in to see them whenever I'm in the area.

. . .

Another dear friend also lives in Fayetteville, Tennessee. E. B. Davis ("call me E. B.") owns the Davis Hardware store on the corner of the town square. It's been an institution in that town for as long as most residents can remember. E. B. and his wife continue to run the establishment, even though they are both in their late seventies. They sell goods the way they were sold back at the turn of the century: nails, bolts, nuts and glass marbles are sold by the pound, scooped from huge metal bins. Long cane fishing poles can be found within the walls of the Davis Hardware store, as can old stoves and bells of every description, from the tiniest cat's bell to cow bells and even replicas of old ship's bells.

• • •

Dows is a small town not far from Britt, Iowa. The week following the hobo convention Dows has a sweet corn festival. For several years I made it a practice to stop in and offer my services during the celebration. The people were very gracious and made me feel at home, I watched some of the kids grow up and came to know many of the citizens very well.

One year the ladies in charge of the food concessions presented a large chocolate cake for me to take with me. It was wrapped in a clear cellophane wrap. I had had a fair amount to drink that evening and decided I would sleep on a bench in the abandoned train depot. I placed the cake at my head and drifted off. The next morning when I woke I discovered that the cake was gone, only the cellophane wrapping remained. Examining the wrap, I discovered two neat holes, one on each side. During the night, mice, who inhabited the depot, had chewed through the wrapping and, piece by piece had carefully removed the cake, leaving the cellophane intact. Sitting on the bench I was reminded of a movie cartoon that had mice silently removing food from under the nose of a sleeping guard. I was overcome with the humor of the vision of those little mice carefully hijacking my cake.

While passing through Rockford, Illinois, I stopped at a small restaurant about eight one Sunday morning to get a set of eggs and coffee. Dressed in my usual road clothes, I looked ragged but clean. A group of people came in all dressed in clothes of the 1920s.

"Are you going to the old timer's day at the Baptist church, too?" one of the group asked me.

I explained that I was just a hobo passing through town.

"Why don't you come along with us; we're going to have some old time preaching, some baptizing in the river, a picnic on the grounds and a lot of mighty good food."

The "lot of mighty good food" was too tempting for me. I agreed to go along.

It was a thoroughly enjoyable day; the people attending took me into their circle, fed me royally, let me take a nap on the grass and made me feel most welcome. As a result of that visit I became close friends with the church's pastor, Jack Zimmer, who for years sent me their church paper and never failed to welcome me whenever I came through town.

Then there was the group I met in DeWitt, Iowa.

I was on my way to Brookings, South Dakota, to attend Hobo Day at South Dakota State University. I had been invited to give a talk on Friday night and then to lead the parade before the Saturday afternoon football game. The annual event was the biggest celebration in the state and had students and others coming to the small town dressed in various forms of hobo dress.

Unfortunately, on the trip out I had run into several days of bad weather, heavy rain storms that had forced me to hole up under bridges and box cars for two or three days. On Thursday night I was still about 500 miles away with no hope of being able to reach Brookings in time for my Friday night speech. I had been hitchhiking and was dropped off on the freeway, in the rain, about two miles from DeWitt in eastern Iowa. I was soaked to the skin and my hip was giving me more pain than it ever had. I felt miserable and very depressed.

On the outskirts of the town I found a small motel. I asked the manager if he would allow me to spend the night there, promising to wash windows or floors or anything else he needed done the next morning. But he was unsympathetic, telling me to "go on into town, there's a preacher there who feeds people."

I went back into the downpour and headed for the center of town. A short distance from the motel I saw an American Legion hall with fifteen or twenty cars parked in the lot. As I was a lifetime member of the Legion, the DeWitt Post was a most welcome refuge from the weather. I went inside.

The instant I limped into the hall the lively conversation all but stopped. I was the sorriest-looking thing they'd ever seen, my old road clothes drenched and sagging, my battered hat drooping over my face. I looked like a drowned chicken.

I stepped to the bar and told the bartender, "I need a drink of bourbon real bad." He gave me an odd look and then asked if I was a member. I told him I was and showed my membership card. As is the custom with the Legion, an out-of-town member's first drink is on the house.

Seated at a nearby table were four or five well-dressed men who appeared to me to be professional or businessmen. From my position at the bar I could hear what they said.

"That old bum came in here and the bartender served him. He isn't supposed to do that."

The others agreed and one called the bartender over to their table.

"Is that old guy a member?" one asked.

"Yes, he's a lifetime member," the bartender replied, satisfying the men.

Now they became curious about me and began wondering aloud just who I was and why I looked the way I did. Finally, one of them came to where I was at the bar.

"Where are you headed?" he inquired.

"Well, I'm headed for Brookings, South Dakota. I'm supposed to be there tomorrow night, but I'm not going to make it now. I hope that I'll be able to get there sometime on Saturday."

The fellow invited me to join the others at their table. I accepted and for the next few hours I told them about my life on the road and they provided me with more bourbon.

I mentioned that I frequently talked to schoolchildren and the men wanted to know what I talked about.

"Mostly about history; the history of the hobos, the history of the railroads, what they've done to help build this country. And I also talk about the drug problem in this country."

"We're having a drug problem in our schools," one of the men stated. "How about talking to our kids?"

"I'd love to, but I've got to leave first thing tomorrow morning and try to get to Brookings in time for the parade on Saturday."

"If we could get you up there tomorrow, would you come back and speak at our school?"

"Yes, I would. But how are you going to get me there tomorrow?"

"We'll get you there," he said firmly.

I spent the night in a back room at the Legion hall and early the next morning two of the businessmen returned and took me to breakfast. They continued to insist that they would get me to Brookings that day but they wouldn't reveal exactly how they planned to do it. After breakfast we got into a car and drove out into the countryside. After a few minutes we pulled into the lane of a farmhouse. Out back I could see several light airplanes parked and there was a sign that indicated that the farmer also was an airplane dealer, a flight instructor and a crop duster.

The men told the farmer/pilot that they wanted me flown to Brookings, South Dakota, and that they would take care of the bill.

About four hours later I called the university from the Brookings airport and they sent someone out to pick me up. I was on campus in plenty of time for my speech.

I marched at the head of the parade the next day and had a marvelous time. I've been to the festival three years and would love to go back anytime they would like to have me.

• • •

Not everyone I came in contact with was influenced by the most praiseworthy or socially accepted motives. In 1980 I was contacted by a fun-loving group in Canada calling themselves the Rhinoceros Party, which had attempted to influence Canadian elections a number of times. American journalists had often criticized Canadian elections as dull. The Rhinoceros Party was out to prove such criticism unfounded. In the last two Canadian elections the Rhinos came dangerously close to gaining power; they won almost 100,000 votes out of 12.5 million cast. Their platform has included such novel approaches to governing as:

Using credit cards to pay off the national debt;
Making the national currency out of bubble gum to facilitate adjusting to inflation and deflation;
Moving the Rocky Mountains to improve the view;
Selling seats in Parliament for ten dollars;
Nationalizing all pay-toilets;
Painting a line with water colors 200 miles offshore to warn the fish when they are in U.S. fishing waters;
Creating world change by reversing the rotation of the earth and repealing the law of gravity;
Promising to answer the question, which came first the chicken or the egg;
Making body language the only language taught in school;
And a firm promise to break all their promises.

I became temporarily involved with this strange group when it decided to run an American candidate against Ronald Reagan in the 1980 presidential election. My name, I was told, would be placed in nomination to become that candidate.

The group invited me to come to Montreal in May 1980 to be present at their nominating convention—which was being held on a downtown street corner—and also advised me that all my expenses for the trip and my stay in Canada would be reimbursed. I should have realized that such a promise would probably fall under their party platform dealing with promises.

But I had never been to Montreal and this unusual political convention appealed to my fondness for the unconventional, so I packed my bindle and boarded a bus in Detroit headed for Quebec.

I had no sooner crossed the border before running into trouble with the authorities. A customs officer took one look at me in my battered old hat, tattered clothes, long beard and walking staff and dragged me off the bus for questioning.

They wanted to know what I was doing in Canada. "To attend the Rhinoceros Party political convention." They then asked how much money I had on me. "Forty dollars." How could I expect to get by in Montreal on just forty dollars? "The people running the convention promised to pay all my expenses." The questioning went on for forty-five minutes before they finally let me go.

The bus had been forced to remain, awaiting the customs office's decision as to whether or not I would be allowed to proceed. The driver was frantic; he was hopelessly behind schedule and the passengers were livid at being made to wait almost an hour for some seedy old bum. It was not a very pleasant bus ride.

I decided that I would turn down the nomination to run against Reagan, and the party finally settled on another hobo who claimed his name was Adam Ybodon—which is "Nobody" misspelled backwards. The party chose to make all 264 card-carrying members of the American branch of the Rhinos nominees for vice president which they argued was the "only way to balance the ticket." Their official campaign slogan became: "Nobody for President . . . Everybody for vice."

They announced their slate at a beer-swilling party at the corner of Duluth and Drolet streets, claiming later that there were 20,000 people in attendance. However, reporters on the scene could count no more than one hundred.

Charlie "The Janitor" McKensie, the Rhinos' campaign chairman, told the party faithful that "we are committing ourselves to Nobody."

Asked to address the crowd, I said simply, "I bring you love and friendship from all the hobos of America." They cheered wildly. The press quoted me as having said, "Being is important, but being important ain't that damned important." I thought the statement was clever and I liked it. I wished that I had said it. but I hadn't; someone else had.

When I attempted to submit my bill for expenses I was told that the party was broke. "We don't have a dime." I'm glad I didn't accept the nomination. The honor would certainly have driven me into bankruptcy.

• • •

Early in 1980 I came to the conclusion that running the iron road was losing some of its wonder. The itch to be on the move had been replaced by the gnawing pain in my right hip, which often made the simple act of sitting by a campfire uncomfortable and walking or other movement difficult. My right leg had become two inches shorter than the left. I had a noticeable limp and had to use my walking staff in order to move about. The joy of being on the road was being dulled, the sense of being independent and carefree didn't seem to matter as much anymore. And I was growing lonely; the number of hobos was steadily declining.

I called one of my daughters occasionally to let my family know I was all right and ask how Wanda was. The years were going by and I was missing the closeness of the family I had longed to have but had sacrificed to stay on the road. Thanksgivings and Christmases were spent at the Salvation Army wherever I happened to be, enjoying a hot turkey dinner with all the trimmings along with other hobos and men without homes or families or roots. These were the saddest times of the year, when my hobo friends could not provide me with the companionship I wanted right then. Many of them were carrying their own lonely burden that could not be lifted in the company of others with the same sorrows.

At those times I was selfishly wallowing in my own self-pity, trying to drown my temporary unhappiness in a river of booze. I thought little of the pain I was causing the ones I loved most. I was completely dulled to the possibility that they might long to have me home, that the glow of their holiday season was being dimmed by my absence.

I had, since 1978, made periodic visits to Toledo where I would call Wanda. She had moved from the apartment we shared before I'd left for the road to a small house in the south part of the city. The house had a small garage and I asked her permission to store some of my possessions there. She agreed and I began spending increasing amounts of time with her. The neighbors had not been aware that Wanda had a husband, assuming that she was a widow or possibly divorced. Once when I was in the backyard I noticed I was getting some strange looks from one of the neighbors. I asked Wanda, "Do these people know about me?" She said that they didn't and I suggested that perhaps she had better let them know who the strange man staying with her was.

Late in 1979, when I commented that I might like to get off the road and come back home, Wanda did not react favorably. Instead she said that she had gotten quite used to not having a man around and wasn't sure that she wanted to go back to the way things were. She partially compromised by saying that she might eventually agree but, in the meantime, we would have to "date" for a while until she made up her mind. To help her reach a conclusion, Wanda consulted with our daughters Alice and Karen. "It's up to you; you should do what you want," was the advice both gave her.

I continued to travel, stopping back every few months. The memories of the good days of hoboing continued to light my way around the country, memories of the many wonderful people I'd met.

. . .

As King of the Hobos I had the pleasant experience of meeting a host of truly wonderful and enjoyable people. I would either receive an invitation to come to where they were or sometimes, as in the case of the veterans in VA hospitals, I traveled for the purpose of seeking them out.

In one case, however, a remarkable, talented and very fine young man spent several months and traveled many miles trying to track me down.

His name was Randall S. Peffer. He was a teacher from New England who spent his summers supplementing his income by writing magazine articles. He learned about me and my travels and decided that I would make an interesting subject. We had corresponded through general-delivery post office addresses, and I agreed to take him with me on a few freight train rides to show him the life of a hobo. But we always seemed to miss each other when he attempted to join me. He was a week late for the Britt convention and was unsuccessful for two months in locating me in Indiana.

I'd mentioned that I would be in Maryland in October and he headed for the Catoctin Mountains where I loved to go each autumn. Railroad crews on the Chessie System told him that I would definitely be coming through and he could find me if he stuck around.

In a small tavern near Camp David, the presidential

retreat, he found a group of elderly men playing mountain music on washboards, one-man bands and bones while others clapped in time to the music or did clog dances on the small dance floor. The tavern was a favorite hangout for newsmen when the president was at the camp. One of my bedrolls still hangs near the ceiling in the tavern.

Peffer asked the group if anyone knew Steam Train Maury.

"He's on the other side of the mountain at the Thurmont Color Festival," one of the group responded.

He went back to the rail yards and asked the yardmaster about a train over the mountain. The yardmaster told him that he could catch the Midnight Special up to the summit and then grab the Thurmont local when it came in to pick up cars. Later a crewman said "You lookin' for Steam Train? I know the old fox. Maybe you can get a dry ride in the caboose or the locomotive. See the engineer when he brings the locomotives up from the round house."

When Peffer climbed into the locomotive cab—to escape a yard bull—the engineer glared at him. But when he explained that he was trying to find me, the engineer broke into a wide grin and told him to get into the second unit—they used two locomotives to pull the train up the mountain—and he would slow down at the summit to allow Peffer to jump off safely.

The conductor joined Peffer in the second unit and talked of how he had worked the Special for forty years and remembered that during the depression the train had run into a blizzard while going up the mountain. There had been carloads of hobos aboard and when the train stalled and started sliding backwards, the hobos had crawled onto the roof of the boxcars and set the individual brakes, keeping the train from rolling back down the mountain and colliding with a passenger train.

At the top of Catoctin, Peffer left the Special and waited three hours in the cold for the westbound local. Finally, a freight agent appeared and invited him into his office to get warm. He recalled how he had met me a number of times and often wished he could join me on the road but that his family responsibilities prevented him from doing so. He called me a "good omen" and said that Peffer just had to meet me. He arranged to get the writer on the local.

Finally, after months of trying and with the help of many people, we were united in Thurmont. Randy has become one of my "friends for life."

In the May, 1978 issue of The *Reader's Digest*, Randall Peffer's article about me appeared. It was titled, "In Search of the Hobo King." It told of his attempts to find me during a summer on the road. It was beautifully done and I felt very honored to be the subject.

In addition to the *Reader's Digest* piece, I was also written up in—of all things—*Penthouse* magazine. They did a beautiful story and a full-color photo spread on several hobos. We were allowed to keep our clothes on, I might add.

In 1979 the Ohio Arts Council awarded Mark Forman, producer/director with WGTE-TV, the Toledo Public Broadcast System station, an individual artists fellowship for the research and the initial filming of a television documentary on my life as a hobo. The central Educational Network provided additional funds to complete the project.

A film crew, consisting of Forman, cinematographer Steven Ashley and Kathy Secrest, production assistant, filmed my appearances at the Britt convention, at a railroad festival in Logansport, Indiana, and at a steam locomotive museum in Bellows Falls, Vermont, as well as at a number of locations in the Toledo area. The result of the film shot was a one-hour documentary titled *The King of the Hobos*, which was first aired on Toledo television on October 14, 1982.

WGTE-TV sent a videocassette of the program to the National Program Service of PBS to see if they were interested in airing the show nationally. On March 22, 1983, *The King of the Hobos* appeared in prime time on PBS stations across the U.S.

The film was selected as the best locally produced documentary for 1983 in Ohio State PBS judging and received a first-place award in the same category in both regional and national PBS contests.

The program is rerun frequently in local and national PBS programming all over the country. Pretty heady stuff for an old dude who had never thought of himself as anything more than a nobody.

• • •

Once Wanda agreed to take me back, I curtailed my road trips considerably. While I still made periodic trips, they were limited to a few days, a weekend or at most four days. I always told her when I was going and when I'd be returning. But I knew that I was simply postponing the inevitable. I was for all purposes a cripple and to continue attempting to ride the freights was asking for trouble; it would be just a matter of time before I would lose my footing, or my knee would buckle and I'd fall beneath the wheels of a railroad car. I may have been irresponsible and undependable but I certainly wasn't stupid; I could, so to speak, see the handwriting on the boxcar.

In the fall of 1980 I slid carefully and painfully from a boxcar to the gravel roadbed in the Toledo railroad yards and slowly limped away. I didn't look back, I couldn't bear to. I had just completed my last year on the iron road and I knew I would never be back to the life that had meant so much to me for almost a half century. My days of riding the freights were over, and I felt a strange sad feeling knowing that I wouldn't be going anymore. It was as though I had just retired from a job I truly loved. But I was now tired of running the line; it was time to give it up.

As I left the freight yards, my thoughts went back fifty years to my first trip on the iron road, to Red McViker and Jimmy Lester OdNeal, to the old 'bos who had taught me and watched over me, to Fry Pan Jack and the Hard Rock Kid and Mountain Dew and to kind, gentle Slow-Motion Shorty. I thought of the warm breeze caressing my face through the open door of a boxcar as the train sped over the flat midwestern plains, of the throbbing of the freight cars and the clicking and clacking of the steel wheels rolling along the seemingly endless steel rails. I heard again the throaty moan and the wheezing complaint of the powerful and majestic steam locomotive that had so endeared itself to hobo and train crew and general public alike that the black, massive, soot-spewing monsters were nonetheless always lovingly referred to by the gentle sobriquet "she."

A flood of images, rushing back from years before, cascaded over me as I made my way out of the freight yards following my final trip; memories of the hard times, of the cold and of the intense heat, of the hunger and the sleepless nights, of fear and pain, of terrible sights and sounds of dying hobos and of brutal bulls. These recollections mingled and fused with the warm visions of the kind, generous, caring people who graciously provided food and shelter and the feeling of pride that came with knowing that we contributed our labors in payment for what was willingly provided us.

All of the memories—good and bad—were somehow *good.*

I had been deeply affected by my experiences on the road, my life had been permanently altered the day I first climbed aboard a boxcar, and now that part of my life was over and done with. I knew I would never be the same.

EPILOGUE

WHEN THE HOBO COMES NO MORE

The longing to ride the freights intensified again following my "retirement." Each spring I felt the desire to ride again. I thought how wonderful it would be to go off for just a week or ten days.

My self-imposed confinement wore at my nerves and aggravated my drinking. I was becoming increasingly argumentative and abusive. Rather than roaming the countryside I was roaming the bars and barroom brawling was becoming a frequent activity.

One afternoon, in a particularly tough Toledo bar, I accidentally bumped a young woman. Although I immediately apologized, she insisted it had been intentional and began egging two male companions to "straighten" me out. I was not in a fighting mood at that point and decided to leave the bar and go across the street to another. But the incident in the first bar ate at me all afternoon as I sat drinking and growing increasingly angry. I knew there were a great deal of illegal drugs being bought and sold in the first bar and it annoyed the hell out of me. Finally, after hours of heavy drinking, I made up my mind that someone should go back in there and clean the place out. I was confident that I was just the one to accomplish such a public service.

Somehow, I got the idea that the men in the first bar were Iranians. I don't know why I thought that, except that the hostages in Teheran were very much in the news just then and, apparently in my stupefied condition, the erroneous connection was made. I called Wanda and told her that I was going to settle the score with the Iranians and insisted that she lock all the doors and not allow anyone but me into the house. I also called a drinking buddy of mine and suggested that he meet me so we could both clean out the offending tavern. But, when he failed to arrive, I staggered across the street alone, entered the bar and began jerking men off bar stools and bashing them. I knocked the first four out cold before the others noticed what was happening and came after me.

There were about twelve men all trying to get in a good punch but the area was too restricted and only one or two at a time could reach me. I was doing pretty well for myself until we rolled out of the bar and into the street. Even then I was able to hold most of them off, fighting in the street and eventually moving across to the second bar.

It was then that I saw the knives come out and I knew that there was a good chance that I'd be killed right there in the street. As I was holding one at bay, smashing him three or four times right in the face and busting his nose, one of the others managed to get behind me and throw his arm around my neck. At that instant the man in front of me swung his knife, stabbing the man behind me in the arm and causing a sudden torrent of blood to gush down the front of my clothes. The stabber thought he had got me and backed off.

I stood there waiting for several seconds, expecting that the man with the knife would make another lunge and might very well get me that time. The rest of the men in the street were crowded around, undecided whether they should make an attack of their own. Just at that moment, the police arrived and broke up the melee.

I looked awful, my clothes were torn, I was mussed up pretty good and I had blood all down the front of my shirt and coat. The cops also believed that I was injured and were prepared to get me to the hospital. Instead, when I told them that the blood wasn't mine but that the men around me were certain to alter that condition, the police decided instead that it would be prudent—not to mention life-saving—to take me out of that situation and drive me home.

Later that night, as I sat alone in our darkened house, I heard a voice, clear and unmistakable. I know there are those who will insist that I was either half asleep or suffering from delirium tremens. But I am absolutely certain of the voice and exactly what it said to me.

"I'll never help you again when you're drunk." Three times the words were said, clearly and distinctly.

I knew that someone had helped me that night. There was no way an old cripple, alone and without assistance, could have fought off twelve young knife-wielding men. Someone had watched over me and had protected me when serious injury and possible death were imminent. And I knew that that someone had helped me at other times when I was in extreme danger. I had always thought that it was simply my quickness, my strength or extremely good luck that had saved me in previous encounters. The night the voice spoke to me I knew that what it was telling me was that I had been assisted in the past, that I had been kept safe but that the protection was being withdrawn. Call it a guardian angel or whatever, the disembodied voice was warning me that if I continued drinking I would be on my own; there would be no further efforts to keep me safe.

The following morning, I told Wanda about the voice and what it had said. I also told her that I was through drinking, and to prove it I went and retrieved a couple of bottles I had secreted in the house and garage and poured them down the kitchen drain.

In a manner of speaking, I guess you could say that I "got religion." Whatever it was, it certainly worked. I've not had a drink since that night.

• • •

I was elected King of the Hobos for the fifth time in 1981. I was also made King of the East for life. I was no longer traveling to the Britt convention by freight car—no one did any longer. Instead I drove a van; I had become a "rubber tire hobo" like all the others.

It was impossible for me to stay at home permanently. So I began accepting many of the invitations I had been receiving; they came from communities holding railroad festivals, from groups holding railroad tours on restored trains, from organizers of fairs and concerts and other area events. I was traveling at my own expense, never asking for a fee of any kind. But my pension money wasn't going very far and the cost of travel, even in a battered old van, was constantly rising.

Finally, I was forced to suggest to those asking that I attend their functions that I would not be able to attend—especially those the farthest away—unless I received some partial reimbursement for oil and gasoline. To my surprise, everyone readily agreed and I was often provided with sufficient funds for food as well as transportation costs.

To get around to the various places where I was being invited to appear I had purchased a van in which I had installed a couch which could be folded down to make a double bed, as well as a small stove that enabled me to do some cooking and provided some heat. It proved very functional during my growing number of trips around the country, but Wanda was now accompanying me on the trips more and more often, and the travel arrangements were not fully adequate for her. I tended to stay up late and sleep late in the morning while Wanda was early to bed and rose early in the morning. With the bed folded down there was very little room in the van to move around. In addition, Wanda didn't like having to use the public restroom facilities along the road.

I realized that some alterations were required to make traveling much more comfortable for both Wanda and myself. We acquired a small used motor home which had two large beds, kitchen facilities that included a cooking stove and an oven, a furnace to provide comfort during winter trips and a bathroom and shower facilities.

Wanda was delighted. Not only would we be able to save money during our travels by doing our own cooking, and not only would we be able to spend the evenings in surroundings that more closely resembled our own home, but she would have a full bathroom rather than having to rely on the public facilities in rest areas and truck stops.

But on the first trip we took with the new vehicle, I stopped to collect a large number of the tree branches I used to fashion walking sticks that I gave as gifts to friends. Much to her annoyance, on the very first morning Wanda got up to use the bathroom, she discovered it was jammed to the ceiling with tree branches, rendering it totally useless to her. I have since made other arrangements to store and transport my collections.

I now alternate between the van and the motor home, using the van when I travel alone and the motor home when Wanda can travel with me on the many trips I make throughout the year.

Having this modern means of movement is a far cry from the days when I had hunkered down on the floor of a boxcar against the bitter cold or had gasped for breath when the heat of summer threatened to boil me alive. Sleeping in a soft, comfortable bed on wheels and cooking my meals over a modern gas range in a dry, windless motor home bears no resemblance to my days on the iron road. But the contrast between what life is like now and what it once was has never been lost on me. The memories of the days and nights spent in the open are brought forcefully back whenever Wanda and I travel today. One such memory is of the night I spent on the campus of Syracuse University in New York.

During my first term as king of the hobos, when I was visiting VA hospitals, I arrived in Syracuse in upstate New York late one night. Throughout the campus of the university were tall buildings that were surrounded by thick hedges. The space between the hedge and the side of the building made excellent sleeping quarters for a hobo. The heavy vegetation provided complete privacy from ground level, as long as the one inside did not stand upright, and the nearness to the building wall made observation from above all but impossible. Of course it was necessary to select hedges that were very thick to fully cut off the view from the ground and to make getting inside sufficiently difficult to discourage others from attempting to force their way in—for whatever reason.

After a comfortable night's sleep on the university grounds, I awoke to hear the voices of students making their way to class. As was my usual practice, I had removed my trousers before wrapping myself in my blanket. I couldn't stand up to put them on without startling the passing students—many of whom, I could tell by their voices, were young women—and perhaps causing them to believe that I was some sort of flasher exposing myself before coeds. I had to stay flat on my back and struggle into my pants and shirt and coat and shoes and then rise up and quickly crash my way through the shrubbery and be on my way before the surprised students could react.

Whenever I was in Washington, D.C., I used the same heavy greenery as the walls of my private sleeping quarters. I had locations right in the middle of the nation's capital where I could sleep undisturbed, that I'm sure some of the street people have not discovered to this day.

Finding a place to sleep comfortably and safely was always a problem when I was a hobo. There have been many times when I had to suffer the elements as best I could. It was not always comfortable, particularly when my hip problem became acute.

I have some very dear friends in Thurmont, Maryland, that I've tried to visit at least once a year. I'm sure the George Wireman family remembers the time I arrived late one night, too late to wake them and ask to be allowed inside to sleep. Instead, I bedded down at their back door, covering myself with a blanket and a large piece of cardboard. A late spring snow fell that night and the next morning the family was surprised to find a sizeable mound of snow at their back door and even more surprised when they found me sleeping soundly beneath it. They brought me in for a nice hot breakfast, amazed at my insistence that I'd spent a very cozy night beneath the snow.

• • •

Because of the amount of publicity I've received over the years, I realize that there are some who believe that I have actively sought this attention. It isn't true; I've never courted publicity for myself; I have no problem with my own ego and I don't look upon myself with a false sense of self-importance. Often I have found myself on television or in the newspapers as the result of something that I never considered newsworthy and had never intended the press to hear.

During the Christmas season of 1986, I found myself the center of attention over controversial children's toys. Since 1981 I had supplemented my Social Security income by working for a Toledo shopping mall as their Santa Claus. I truly loved being Santa for the kids; Wanda made most of my costume, and my white beard and big round belly made me a natural candidate for the job. One year a local television station took a group of children around to all the area shopping centers where there was a Santa and then asked them to select the most realistic. I won easily.

But by 1985 I had become very concerned about the type of toys that were being marketed. To me they seemed to be evil, satanic, anti-Christian toys that encouraged violence. I was particularly troubled by the so-called Masters of the Universe line of action figures and by the Rambo dolls. I felt that Christ was the master of the universe and not a bunch of ugly, overbuilt and scantily dressed men and women. I believed that this type of toy was hardly suitable for impressionable children and I cringed each time a small boy or girl would climb on my lap and tell me that they wanted this kind of toy for Christmas.

I realized that to continue with my practice of being Santa Claus for the mall I would have to tell the kids that they shouldn't have this kind of toy and shouldn't even ask for one. I had no doubt that word would quickly get back to the shopkeepers in the mall and ultimately to the large toy manufacturers that spend millions each year in advertising such toys. It wouldn't take long before there would be a confrontation between myself and the directors of the shopping mall. I didn't want an ugly incident to mar the Christmas spirit. And so I simply told them that I could not, in good conscience, continue as their Santa. They understood and harbored no ill will toward me—at least not then.

Word spread immediately through the mall and to the local TV stations and then the wire services and then to the ABC and CNN news networks. Headlines proclaiming: "Santa Quits" sprang up everywhere. Within a few days I was swamped with telephone calls, letters, telegrams and postcards supporting my stand against violent toys. I received phone calls from as far away as Alaska and Hawaii and Australia and letters from halfway around the world. I heard from children who wrote to "Santa Claus, Toledo, Ohio," agreeing with my position and asking me not to stop being Santa.

I continue to be Santa at Christmas time for private parties as well as visiting hospitals, crippled children's homes and orphanages; I ride in area parades and appear on television. In 1987, in my full Santa Claus costume, I appeared as "guest co-anchor" with Jeff Heitz on the eleven o'clock Christmas Eve newscast on Toledo's Channel 11 (just before I left on my rounds, of course). I was very impressed with Jeff, one of Toledo's most respected and popular newscasters. He made me feel very comfortable and never once talked down to me or appeared annoyed having an outright amateur share the studio with him. He later said that he wouldn't consider talking down to me. "No one talks down to Santa Claus," he said.

Being Santa has been an important part of my life. And being the King of the Hobos has given real meaning to my existence and has caused me to feel that I've contributed in some small measure to our society. I have tried to keep the spirit of the hobo alive, to bring his history and his message to those who knew him not or understood him little.

I have thoroughly enjoyed my travels around the country. I like to think that my participation in the many railroad festivals and fairs and expositions that have sprung up over the past twenty years or so has helped to foster these celebrations and has encouraged other communities to establish them. The enthusiastic reception I've received from the public has given me the will to go on year after year.

The convention in Britt is still one of the highlights of my year. The date has been changed; the convention will now be held the second week in August. I would like to see a time when a hobo special train could be run into Britt for the convention, when everyone who wished to could ride the special, dressed as hobos to keep the hobo's image as well as his memory alive.

I can now take to the road in relative comfort, and not just because of a motor home or a van. In 1986 I had an operation to replace my ailing hip with metal and plastic. My right leg, which had been two inches shorter than the left, is now of normal size; the pain is gone and I walk without a noticeable limp. Were it not for a troublesome knee—which will have to have some medical attention soon—I could easily ride the freights again. Unfortunately they are becoming too few now . . . like the hobos.

Today I sit in the lengthening shadows of my life. I hear in the distance the unmistakable call of the Westbound, and I wait and watch with growing sadness the approach of the midnight of the hobo, of a world without the kindly, compassionate gentleman of the road who, without conscious effort, brought to our culture a gentle philosophy of honesty and goodness and a concern for nature and the environment and the beauty of an unspoiled land.

I live with the hope that, when the Westbound carries me away, I will have left behind me some tangible mark that, like the hobo signs and signals of my youth, will serve to guide the generations to come along the path of the old hobo, the path of gentleness, peace and love.

The hobo is almost never seen today at the back doors of America; they have been largely relegated to railroad festivals and fairs and, occasionally, to senior citizens' homes. I sincerely hope that it will not become their lot to be viewed as a sideshow attraction; they have contributed too much to the history of this country to suffer that fate. It should be said, however, that, by his very nature, it is the mild-mannered, solitary hobo who would be the last to raise his voice in complaint about what might be done to his memory. After all, most of his life has been spent in being the brunt of the thoughtless actions by those who would not or could not understand his unusual lifestyle.

But today we live in a much more enlightened time; people are more willing to cast out old prejudices and even to refuse to adopt them in the first place. We are a more curious people; we are a more compassionate group. Now is the time to learn about the hobo and his love of nature and his fear that the environment could be destroyed. Even though he may soon pass from the scene, the hobo has a legacy that all might share and profit from. There isn't much time remaining; the hobo is an endangered species; like the dinosaur, he will become extinct. Sadly, we will soon see the day when the hobo comes no more.

The places along the riverbanks, where once the hobo jungles were found, are deserted now, probably forever; the campfires are cold, never to be rekindled. On warm summer nights, when once the hobo's songs of the road lifted to the soft breezes, to be interrupted occasionally by the low, mournful call of a steam locomotive's whistle, there is now only stillness or the intrusive whine from nearby interstate highways and, perhaps, the shrill blast of a diesel engine's horn.

The gentle glow that once beckoned a weary traveler to come into the hobo circle for rest and warmth and a bite to eat has disappeared from the iron road, and the men who populated these havens are rapidly vanishing as well, taking with them a tradition and a history that will never be repeated . . . if only it could be remembered.

ORANGE COUNTY LIBRARY SYSTEM